Wilfur Crafts

Little pilgrim songs

For primary classes and singing in the home

Wilfur Crafts

Little pilgrim songs
For primary classes and singing in the home

ISBN/EAN: 9783337266103

Printed in Europe, USA, Canada, Australia, Japan

Cover: Foto ©Thomas Meinert / pixelio.de

More available books at **www.hansebooks.com**

LITTLE PILGRIM SONGS:

FOR

Primary Classes and Singing in the Home.

A NEW COLLECTION OF

SACRED AND SECULAR SONGS,

(Including Motion Songs.)

TOGETHER WITH A NUMBER OF

Services for Anniversary Occasions,

ARRANGED FOR THIS BOOK,

BY

MRS. WILBUR F. CRAFTS AND HUBERT P. MAIN.

———•———

New · York · and · Chicago :
PUBLISHED BY BIGLOW & MAIN.

SINGING IN THE PRIMARY CLASS.

As the Jewish pilgrims, on their way to the feasts at Jerusalem, had their "Songs of the going up" (songs of degrees), with which they cheered their own hearts and praised God as they journeyed, so the Little Pilgrims on their way to the Heavenly Jerusalem should also have their songs of joy, comfort and praise.

AIM.

To teach the children to worship God in song, and not for their own pleasure, nor the entertainment of friends.

It is, therefore, necessary that they should understand the words they sing, and be in the spirit of the song. Sacred song will fail of its purpose if little ones blindly sing, "Black tidies," for "Glad tidings," or "Three five us again," for "Revive us again."

TIME.

Certainly not over one fourth of the session should be spent in singing. It should not be done at one time, but at intervals throughout the session, in order to make restful episodes.

NUMBER.

It is better to keep the children well practiced in a few songs, than to have them half-know a large number. Ten, or at most twelve songs, will form as large a collection as little children can keep in practice. They should be taught one new song each month, and about as often one that is worn out should be dropped.

TEACHING A NEW SONG.

1. Read over two lines, or at most one verse ; talk about it ; illustrate its meaning on the blackboard, or by stories or pictures.
2. Let the children repeat the words.
3. Have the air played on the piano or organ.
4. Let the teacher sing it alone.
5. Let the children sing it with the teacher, learning one or two lines at a time.
6. Let them try to sing it without the teacher.
7. Get the children to promise to sing the new piece at home through the week.

THE QUALITIES OF A GOOD SONG FOR CHILDREN.

Gospel truth instead of jingling, meaningless rhymes.
Simplicity in words and music.
Cheerful and bright.
No high notes ; seldom above E, and not often that high.

LESSON SONGS.

At least one song in each lesson should be in harmony with the lesson taught. As often as possible let a church hymn be selected. Such selections should be printed on the lesson papers of the children, and may be sung by those who can read, even if no attempt is to be made on future Sundays to repeat them.*

DIRECTIONS FOR MOTION SONGS.

Frequent inquiries from Primary teachers for "Motion Songs," have influenced the authors of this book to include many such songs in this collection. Back of the inquiries of the teachers for Motion Songs are these facts:

Children delight to suit their actions to their words ; that children are helped to understand better what they sing when motions are used. Children are thus provided with the necessary changes of position, in order to prevent restlessness.

This method of singing, the Sunday School has learned from the Kindergarten, where the songs are hardly without exception of this character.

It is as natural for children to imitate, or in some way represent what they are singing about, as it is for birds to fly. Not only do the children themselves enjoy it, but their friends take pleasure in seeing them.

In teaching songs with motions, three things should be observed by the teacher:

1st. To be perfectly familiar with the words and motions, so that no book will be needed.

2d. To be the leader. To do just what the children are expected to do, so that they need only be told, "Watch me, and do just as I do."

3d. To use the left hand when the children are expected to use their right hands; this is necessary from the opposite position of the teacher.

The following directions will speak for themselves. The whole collection of songs has been considered, and whenever it seemed desirable, motions have been adapted.

"CRADLE SONG." p. 18.

During the singing of the first and second verses, require arms to be extended in front, but curved rather than straight, and let them be swayed from right to left and back again, to represent the rocking of a cradle. No motions for the last verse.

"QUESTIONS AND ANSWERS." p. 23.

v. 1. "Her narrow hole to bore"—boring imitated with the index finger of right hands.

v. 2. "The sparrow builds her clever nest"—right and left hands extended in front, side by side, palms uppermost, fingers curved to represent a nest.

v. 3. "The busy bee to fly"—pointing in several directions successively with index finger of right hand.

v. 4. "If they pray"—hands folded as in prayer.

"JESUS ONCE WAS A LITTLE CHILD." p. 24.

v. 1. "Like me"—children point to themselves with the index finger of their right hands.

* "Normal Outlines for Primary Teachers," by Mrs. W. F. Crafts.

v. 2. " He grew as children do "—right hands not far from the floor at first, and gradually raised to about four feet, as if measuring the growth of children.

v. 3. " His heavenly home"—pointing upward.

" RAINDROPS, BIRDS AND FLOWERS." p. 50.

v. 1. " Rain drops ! rain drops ! " hands raised and shaken as if rain were dropping from the finger-tips. " We come to make the grasses grow," tapping on a hard surface to represent the pattering of rain. " Our Father in the heavens,"— hands raised aloft and eyes looking up, in an attitude of ascribing praise. Chorus—hands folded across the breast.

" LITTLE ONES LIKE ME." p. 52.

" Little ones like me."—Children touch their breasts with the index finger of their left hands whenever these words occur.

" MANSIONS ARE PREPARED." p. 53,

" For me."—Each time when this is sung, the children should point to themselves with the index finger of their right hands.

" GOD HAS MADE ALL THINGS." p. 54.

v. 1. No motions. Chorus—index finger of right hand pointing upwards.

v. 2. " Each little flower that opens"—finger tips of left and right hands touching, and gradually opening from the wrist as a hinge. " He made their tiny wings"— hands raised and spread to represent the flying of a bird.

v. 3. "The purple-headed mountain"—arms raised, finger tips of right and left hands touching, to represent a mountain. " The river running by"—right hands waving slowly from left to right.

v. 4. " He gave us eyes," etc.—hands touching eyes. "And lips"—index finger of left hand touching lips. " The sunset"—left hands extended towards West. "And the morning"—right hands extended towards East.

" GUARD, MY CHILD." p. 59.

" Guard, my child, thy tongue." While singing this line, children point to their tongues with index finger of the right hand.

v. 2. " Guard, my child, thine eyes."—Children touch their eyes lightly, as they sing this line. at the beginning and ending of the verse ; hands in laps while the rest of the verse is sung.

v. 3. " Guard, my child, thine ear."—Children touch both right and left ears.

v. 4. " Ear," (first and last line), touch ears ; " Eye" ; touch eyes ; " and tongue" point to tongues.

" THE CHILD'S GIFT TO GOD." p. 63.

v. 1. " Two little eyes"—touch eyes lightly. " Two little ears"—fingers on ears. " Two little feet"—point to feet. "Hands to serve Him"—hands extended horizontally in front.

" CHILDREN'S THANKS." p. 67.

v. 1. Left hands on heart when singing " With gladsome hearts ;" both hands raised aloft when singing "Our praise we bring ; " hands folded across the breast when singing "This is the children's King ; " hands folded as in prayer when sing ing " For this we thank Thee, Lord."

v. 2. No motions.

v. 3. Hands folded and heads bowed, as in prayer, during the singing of the whole verse.

"SAVIOUR, WHO THY FLOCK." p. 81.

To be sung as a prayer, with folded hands and closed eyes, or even in a kneeling posture.

"A WONDERFUL HOUSE." p. 82.

v. 1. "A wonderful house have I"—hands swept from the head towards the feet. "With windows"—finger-tips on both eyes ; "To see the sky"—looking upward; "And keepers"—both hands raised slightly, and fingers spread ; "The door"—touch lips. "Tuneful harp"—point to vocal cords. "Golden bowl "—both hands on heads. "Silver thread"—left hands run along spines (spinal cord).

v. 2. "A fountain"—right hands on hearts. "A pitcher"—hands on lungs, "Strong men"—hands on thighs. "The keepers must work," etc.—hands raised and fingers spread. "The harp"—point to vocal cords. "The windows"—eyes looking up to the sky. "Strong men walk His ways"—treading first on one foot and then on the other.

v. 3. " Better house"—hands swept from the head to the feet. "Above, in Jesus' home"— index finger of right hand pointing upwards.

"THE DOVE AND THE RAVEN." p. 85.

v. 1. " In a baby's breast"—hands on hearts.

v. 2. "All the smiles and all the dimples"—hands on cheeks.

v. 3. " Drove the gentle birdie"—hands pushed out forcefully from the hearts.

v. 4. " To its nest again"—hands gently folded on the hearts.

"EASTER SONG " p. 87.

v. 1. "Snow-drops"—hands held in front, in a horizontal position. "Lift your timid heads" hands raised perpendicularly from the wrists. "How he rose," etc. arms gradually rising until their full length is reached. Do so each time these words are sung as a chorus.

v. 2. "Ring your bells, and tell the story"—right arms in front, raised a little, and curved to represent a stem of lilies ; imitate the ringing of bells by shaking the hand in regular motion up and down.

v. 3. "Waken, sleeping butterflies"—right and left hands, palm opposite palm, finger-tips touching, fingers slightly curved, to represent the chrysalis. "Burst your narrow prison"—hands opened slightly, with quick motion. "Spread your golden wings"—hands open, thumb to thumb. "Spread your golden wings and rise"—hands raised above, and moved to represent flying.

Several pages of secular songs for use in the day school and home circle will be found, with and without motions.

The greater portion of the music has been written and arranged for this collection.

We are especially indebted to Mrs. M. G. Kennedy for two services and useful suggestions ; also, to Rev. Robert Lowry, II. R. Palmer, Mus. Doc., W. H. Doane, Mus. Doc., Theo. F. Seward, B. Carl Unseld, Mrs. V. J. Kent, Mrs. Jos. F. Knapp, and others, for new and valuable contributions.

Mrs. WILBUR F. CRAFTS,
HUBERT P. MAIN.

November 10, 1883.

CLASSIFIED INDEX.

LITTLE PILGRIM SONGS.

HAPPY LITTLE PILGRIMS.

GRACE J. FRANCES.   HUBERT P. MAIN.

1. Happy   little   pilgrims,   We should ne'er be sad; For the love of
2. In that land so love - ly   Everything is bright; There will be no
3. Not a - lone we jour-ney   To the mansions fair; Je - sus is our

Je-sus, Makes His children glad. Happy lit-tle pilgrims,   Go - ing
sorrow, There will be no night.
Shepherd, He will lead us there.

on our way, To   a   land of beau-ty, Singing all   the day.

8   JESUS, DEAR, I COME TO THEE.

F. J. C.

FANNY J. CROSBY.

1. Je - sus, dear, I come to Thee, Thou hast said I may.
   Je - sus, dear, I learn of Thee, In Thy word di - vine.

Tell me what my life should be, Take my sins a - way.
Ev - ery promise there I see, May I call it mine.

Chorus.

Je - sus, hear my humble song, I am weak, but Thou art strong;

Gently lead my soul a - long, Help me come to Thee

2 Jesus, dear, I long for Thee,
Long Thy peace to know,
Grant those purer joys to me,
Earth can ne'er bestow
Jesus, dear, I wait for Thee
When my heart is sad,
Thou wilt kindly speak to me,
Thou wilt make me glad.

3 Jesus, dear, I trust in Thee,
Trust Thy tender love,
There's a happy home for me,
With Thy saints above
Jesus, I would come to Thee,
Thou hast said I may,
Tell me what my life should be,
Take my sins away.

BLESSED, BLESSED JESUS.

Anon.

Wm. B. Bradbury.

Moderato.—Teacher.

Scholars.

1. Who was in a manger laid? Je - sus, blessed Je - sus;
2. Who can rob the grave of gloom? Je - sus, blessed Je - sus;
3. Who will give us sweet-est rest? Je - sus, blessed Je - sus:

Teacher.

Scholars.

Who for money was betrayed? Je - sus, blessed Je - sus.
Who can raise us from the tomb? Je - sus, blessed Je - sus.
Who in heaven shall we love best? Je - sus, blessed Je - sus.

Teacher.

Who will lead us eve - ry day, Who will hear us when we pray?
When be-fore the Judge we wait. Who will o - pen heaven's gate?
At His feet our crowns we'll fling, While with rapt'rous songs we sing.

Scholars.

All.

Je - sus, Je - sus all the way; Je - sus, blessed Je - sus.
Je - sus Christ, our Ad-vo-cate; Je - sus, blessed Je - sus.
Je - sus Christ, our Saviour King, Je - sus, blessed Je - sus.

O WHEN WE REMEMBER.

FANNY J. CROSBY.   B. CARL UNSELD.

1. O when we re - mem-ber the words of our Lord, How
2. When fa - thers and moth-ers, His bless-ing to ask, Their
3. We thank our dear Shepherd for all He has done, We

grate-ful and hap - py are we, That, speaking of
lit - tle ones brought to His knee; He took them up
thank Him that mer - cy is free; And, O how we -
D.S.—He gath-ers the

children He ten - der - ly said, "For - bid not their
gent - ly, and smil - ing He said, "For - bid not their
thank Him that children may come, And heirs of His
lambs in His kind, lov - ing arms, And car - ries them

FINE. CHORUS.

com-ing to Me." Ah, well may we cling to our
com-ing to Me."
kingdom may be.
all the day long.

D. S.

Shepherd and Friend, His goodness may well be our song;

MERRY, CHIMING BELLS.

FANNY J. CROSBY. W. F. SHERWIN.

1. Mer-ry, mer-ry chiming bells, Clear and sweet their carol swells;
2. In a manger far a-way, Once the in-fant Sav-iour lay;
3. Let the glorious tidings fly, Angels sing and earth re - ply;

Joy - ful news that mu-sic tells—Glo - ry in the high - est.
We will sing His birth to-day, Glo - ry in the high - est.
Glo - ry be to God on high! Glo - ry in the high - est.

CHORUS. *All the School.*

Glo - ry be to God on high, Glo - ry in the highest!

12 CHILD'S PRAYER.

Rev. J. N. FOLWELL.   Rev R. LOWRY.

1. Fa - ther, a - bove, Thou God of love, To Thee I give
2. On this new day, To Thee I pray; Be Thou my guide,
3. My eyes di - rect, My ears pro - tect, From words and scenes
4. And at sun - set, Let no re - gret Of mis-spent time,

Thanks that I live; All thro' the night, Till broad day-light,
Walk by my side; Make me with - in All free from sin,
Thy Book condemns; My tongue restrain From things profane;
O Lord, be mine; Still let me share Thy ten - der care,

CHORUS.

Thou hast kept me While I have slept. For this I plead,
And fix my place With-in Thy grace.
My hands and feet Both guide and keep.
And at life's end To Thee as - cend.

And all I need. Thro' Christ, my Lord, The Son of God.

Miss M. A. Baker.   H. R. Palmer, by per.

1. Love God with thy heart,   Let ev' - - ry part, Throb
2. Love God with thy mind,   In Him shalt thou find, All
3. Love God with thy strength, Then may'st thou at length; Thy

warm-ly and true, As His does for you, God's heart throbs for you.
wisdom and might; All knowledge and light, God's word giveth light.
brother's soul win, From folly and sin, God's love saves from sin.

CHORUS.

The great law is love, Christ came from a - bove, To

teach it below, 'Mid earth's weal and woe, Christ-love healeth woe.

14 HAPPY WE, YOUNG AND FREE.

GRACE J. FRANCES.

HUBERT P. MAIN.

1. Hap - py we, young and free, Full of joy and glad-ness,
2. Hap - py we, young and free, Laughing, play-ing, sing-ing,
3. Hap - py we, young and free, Heart and voic - es rais-ing;

Eyes so bright, hearts so light, Nev - er dream of sad-ness;
While the hours, bright with flow'rs, Merry flight are wing-ing;
For His love, from a - bove, Our Re - deem - er prais-ing;

Clouds we know, come and go, Yet we do not mind them,
He, whose eye, ev - er nigh, Lov - ing watch is keep - ing,
May His smile, all the while, Sweet-ly beam-ing o'er us,

Tho' they stay, all the day, Sun-beams hide be - hind them.
Guards us still, safe from ill When we all are sleep - ing.
Cheer our way, night and day, Go - ing on be - fore us.

Earnestly.

1. Je - sus is our Shepherd, Wip-ing eve - ry tear; Fold-ed
2. Je - sus is our Shepherd, Well we know His voice, How its
3. Je - sus is our Shepherd, For the sheep He bled; Eve - ry

in His bo - som, What have we to fear? On - ly let us
gentlest whis-per Makes our heart re-joice! Ev - en when He
lamb is sprinkled With the blood He shed. Then on each He

fol - low Whither He doth lead, To the thirsty des - ert,
chid-eth Ten - der is His tone, None but He shall guide us,
set-teth His own se - cret sign: "They that have my Spir-it,

Or the dew-y mead.
We are His a - lone.
These, said He, "are mine."

4 Jesus is our Shepherd,
　　Guided by His arm,
　Though the wolves may ravin,
　　None can do us harm.
　When we tread death's valley,
　　Dark with fearful gloom,
　We will fear no evil,
　　Victors o'er the tomb.

HARK! THE LARK IS SINGING.

ANON.

THOS. CRAMPTON, arr.

1. Hark! the lark is sing - ing, In the clear blue sky;
2. Lit - tle lark what is it Makes your heart so gay?

Now I scarce can see him, He has flown so high:
Do you love the sun-shine, This bright, sunny day?

Yet his glad song float - ing Downward still to earth,
Do you know who made us, And the earth so fair?

Shows his lit - tle heart is Full of joy and mirth.
Have you flown to thank Him For His love and care?

SING ALWAYS.

FANNY J. CROSBY.　　　　　　　　WM. F. SHERWIN.

1. Sing with a tune-ful spir - it, Sing with a cheerful lay,
2. Sing when the heart is troubled, Sing when the hours are long,
3. Sing in the vale of shadows, Sing in the hour of death,

Praise to thy great Cre - a - tor, While on the pilgrim way.
Sing when the storm-cloud gathers; Sweet is the voice of song.
And when the eyes are clos - ing, Sing with the lat-est breath.

Sing when the birds are waking, Sing with the morning light;
Sing when the sky is darkest, Sing when the thunders roll;
Sing till the heart's deep longings Cease on the oth-er shore;

Sing in the noon-tide's golden beam, Sing in the nush of night.
Sing of a land where rest re-mains, Rest for the weary soul.
Then with the countless numbers there, Sing on, for-ev - er-more!

CRADLE SONG.

Anna Warner.   T. E. Perkins.

1. O lit - tle child! lie still and sleep; Je - sus is here. Thou
2. O lit - tle child! be still and rest.—He sweetly sleeps Whom
3. O lit - tle child! when thou must die, Fear nothing then. But

need'st not fear; No one need fear whom God doth keep By
Je - sus keeps.—And in the morn-ing wake so blest. His
say "A - men" To God's command, and qui - et lie In

day or night. By day or night; Then lay thee down in
child to be. His child to be; Love eve - ry one, but
His kind hand. In His kind hand, Till He shall say, "Dear

slum-ber deep. Till morning light. Till morning light.
love Him best.—He first loved thee. He first loved thee.
child, come, fly To heaven's bright land. To heaven's bright land.

Motion Song—See p. 3.   Copyrighted, 1870, in "Songs of Salvation," by T. E. Perkins

'TIS NOT FAR TO JESUS.

FANNY J. CROSBY.

W. H. DOANE.

1. 'Tis not far to Je - sus, He is eve - ry - where,
2. 'Tis not far to Je - sus, No, 'tis ver - ry near;
3. 'Tis not far to Je - sus; O how glad we are;
4. If we want to love Him, Let us go and pray;

Watching o'er His child - ren With a ten - der care.
He is all a - round us, He is with us here.
'Tis not far to Je - sus, He is eve - ry - where.
Then our hearts can find Him, Now this ver - y day.

REFRAIN.

Ear - ly if we seek Him, Ear - ly we shall find Him;

'Tis not far to Je - sus, He is eve - ry - where.

Copyright, 1880, by Biglow & Main.

GLORY TO THE FATHER GIVE.

J. MONTGOMERY.   Mrs. Jos. F. KNAPP.

1. Glo - ry   to   the   Fa - ther give,   Glo - ry,   glo - ry!
2. Glo - ry   to   the   Sav-iour give,   Glo - ry,   glo - ry!

God   in   whom   we   move   and   live,   move   and   live;
Christ   our   Proph - et,   Priest   and   King, Priest   and   King!

Children's pray'rs He deigns to hear, Glo - ry!   glo - ry! glo - ry!
Children, raise your sweetest strains, Glo - ry!   glo - ry! glo - ry!

Children's songs de-light   His ear,   Glo - ry! glo - ry! glo - ry!
To   the Lamb for He   was slain, Glo - ry! glo - ry! glo - ry!

CHORUS.

Glo - ry! glo - ry! In the high - est, glo - ry!

Glo - ry! glo - ry! To the Lord our King!

JESUS KNOWS.

V. J. K.   Mrs. V. J. KENT, by per.

1. All   our lit - tle heart-aches, All   our joys and woes,
2. And   our ev - ery ac - tion Is   to   Je - sus known;
3. When we play or stu - dy, When we wake or sleep,
4. He   will al - ways guide us, Lis - ten to our prayers;

All our hopes and wish - es, Je - sus says He knows.
From the time we're lit - tle, Till we're ful - ly grown.
He de - lights to bless us, And His children keep.
For the lov - ing Sav - iour, For His children cares.

22 CHILDREN MAY COME TO THE SAVIOUR.

H. R. P.

H. R. Palmer, by per.

1. Je - sus loves lit - tle children; He is their Friend; His
2. Je - sus now doth en - treat you; List to His voice, Oh,
3. Je - sus now doth command you; Do not de - lay; Oh,

aid He will lend, Like a Shepherd He'll lead them; Come to Him
hear and re - joice; He is read - y to meet you; Little ones
haste to o - bey; Dangers dark will surround you, If from your

CHORUS.

children, to - day. Children may come, children may come,
turn not a - way.
Saviour you stray.

Children may come to the Sav - iour, Children may come.

Children may come, Children may come and be saved.

QUESTIONS AND ANSWERS.

ANON.   HUBERT P. MAIN.

1. *Who* show'd the lit-tle ant the way Her narrow hole to bore,
2. The Sparrow builds her clev-er nest Of wool, and hay, and moss;

And spend the pleasant summer day In lay-ing up her store?
Who told her how to weave it best, And lay the twigs a-cross?

3 *Who* taught the busy bee to fly
   Among the sweetest flowers;
   And lay his feast of honey by,
   To eat in winter hours?

4 'Twas God who showed them all the way,
   And gave their little skill;
   And teaches children if they pray,
   To do His holy will.

MOTION SONG—See page 3. Copyright, 1883, by Bigl.w & Main.

24   JESUS ONCE WAS A LITTLE CHILD.

J. R. M.

JAMES R. MURRAY, by per.

Moderato.

1. Je - sus once was a lit - tle child, A   lit - tle child like
2. Je - sus once was a lit - tle child, And He grew as chil - dren

me,   And He   was   pure, and meek, and mild, As a
do,   While His mother taught Him lov-ing - ly, To be

lit - tle child should be;   He   played as   lit - tle
gen - tle, kind and   true;   O - ver   the   fields of

children play, The   pleasant games of   youth,   But He
Beth - le - hem, With playmates He   did roam,   But He

MOTION SONG—See page 3.

nev - er got vexed if the game went wrong, And He
nev - er would fret and scold and pout, When His

al - ways spoke the truth. So, lit-tle children, let
moth-er called Him home.

REFRAIN.

you and I, Try to be like Him, try, try, try.

3 Jesus once was a little child,
  He came to us to show
The way to His pure, sweet life above,
  From our sinful life below;
We must be, and do, and love like Him,
  Be kind, all evil shun,
And He'll bring us all to His heavenly home,
  When our life-work is done.

26 OUR HEARTS ARE YOUNG AND JOYOUS.

Arr. by F. J. C.   WM. B. BRADBURY.

1. Our hearts are young and joy-ous, 'Tis spring-time with us now;
2. O, can we e'er for - get Him Who is so good and kind?
3. O, help us, then, dear Sav-iour, To give our hearts to Thee;

The dew of life's bright morning Is fresh up - on each brow;
No, rath-er would we love Him With all our heart and mind;
Let us, in youth's glad morning, Thy loved dis - ci - ples be!

The word to us seems pleas-ant, With love its joys to share;
But we can nev-er love Him Till we are pure with - in;
Then safe up - on Thy bo - som Our hearts may e'er re - cline;

God in His ten-der kind - ness Hath made it ver - y fair.
The pre-cious blood of Je - sus Must wash us first from sin.
And, 'mid the joys e - ter - nal We ev - er shall be Thine.

DEAR SAVIOUR, MAY THY BLESSING. 27

FANNY J. CROSBY. THEO. F. SEWARD.

1. Dear Saviour, may Thy blessing   At-tend Thy ho - ly word,
2. An - oth-er day is   bear-ing   Our record   up to Thee,
3. And now, di - vine Re - deem-er,   From whom all blessings flow,

D.S.—*peace which pass - eth   knowledge,   Thy love to   us   im - part;*

FINE.

Which thro' Thy ten-der   mer-cy, This day our ears have heard;
0   deep, and   earn-est question, What will that rec-ord be?
Pro - tect and guide our footsteps, Go   with us where we   go,

A - bide, O   gra - cious Sav - iour,   A - bide in   ev - ery   heart.

Im - press its truth up - on   us, And help us now   to   say,
If thought and mind have wandered, Our weakness, Lord, forgive,
And   if   Thy will, dear Sav-iour,   That we should meet a-gain,

D.S.

That with Thy grace to help us, We'll choose the better way.   *Thy*
And help us from this mo-ment A bet - ter life   to   live.
Thy name shall have the glo-ry For-ev - er more, A - men.

Copyright, 1883, by Biglow & Main

28   LITTLE ONES.

V. J. K.   German Melody, by per.

1. Ver-y lit-tle ones are we,   Com-ing Je-sus,
2. Ver-y lit-tle do we know,   As the moments
3. Ver-y lit-tle can we do,   On-ly to be

un - to Thee;   Wilt Thou lov-ing-ly, Look ap -
come and go,   Pass-ing fast a - way, Wilt Thou
good and true;   List-'ning to Thy voice, In Thy

prov - ing - ly;   Suf - fer them to come, said He.
eve - ry day   Help us all to wis - er grow?
love re - joice, With our sin - ful hearts made new.

4 Very little time have we,
Swiftly comes eternity;
Oh! be Thou our Guide,
Ever by Thy side,
May we feel security.

GRACE J. FRANCES.   HUBERT P. MAIN.

1. Ear - ly, O my Sav - iour, I have come to Thee,
2. Ear - ly have I sought Thee, May Thy pres-ence near,
3. Dai - ly I am trust - ing, Trusting in Thy love,

Hear my sup - pli - ca - tion, Grant Thy grace to me.
Ban-ish ev - ery sor - row, Con - quer ev - ery fear.
Lay-ing up my treas-ure For a life a - bove.

CHORUS.

On Thy strength de-pend - ing, All things I can do,

Ev - ery toil and tri - al Thou wilt bring me through.

HARK! THE VOICE.

MARY B. SLEIGHT. H. R. PALMER, by per.

1. Hark! the voice of Je - sus call - ing, "Fol - low me,
2. Who will heed the ho - ly man-date, "Fol - low me,
3. Hark - en, lest He plead no long - er, "Fol - low me,

fol - low me!" Soft - ly thro' the si - lence fall - ing,
fol - low me!" Leav - ing all things at His bid - ding,
fol - low me!" Once a - gain, oh, hear Him call - ing,

"Fol - low, fol - low me!" As of old, He called the
"Fol - low, fol - low me!" Hark! that ten-der voice en -
"Fol - low, fol - low me!" Turn-ing swift at Thy sweet

fish - ers, When He walk'd by Gal - i - lee, Still His
treat-ing, Mar - i - ners on life's rough sea, Gent - ly,
sum-mons, Ev - er-more, O Christ, would we, For Thy

pa - tient voice is pleading, "Fol - low, fol - low me!"
lov - ing - ly re - peat-ing, "Fol - low, fol - low me!"
love all else for - sak-ing, "Fol - low, fol - low me!"

GOD'S BLESSED BOOK.

ANON.   W. T. ROGERS.

1. What book ought I to love the best, And on its truths se -
2. What points me to the Lamb of God, To trust in His a -

cure - ly rest? The Bi - ble, the Bi - ble, God's
ton - ing blood? The Bi - ble, &c.

blessed book, the Bi - ble.

3 What warns me to abstain from sin,
And tends to make me pure within?
   The Bible, &c.

4 What teaches me to love my foe,
And acts of kindness to him show?
   The Bible, &c.

32   LITTLE THINGS.

GRACE J. FRANCES.   HUBERT P. MAIN.

1. Time is made of lit - tle moments, Moments make the hours,
2. Lit - tle rays in beauty shin-ing, Make the morning bright,
3. Lit - tle snow-flakes, white and downy, Cov - er all the hills,

Lit - tle rain-drops gent-ly fall - ing, Bring refreshing show'rs;
Lit - tle deeds of love may sparkle In a crown of light;
Lit - tle chains the frost is weaving Bind the brooks and rills;

From the a - corn by the way-side Comes a stately tree,—
Lit - tle voi - ces, when they mingle In a grateful song,
Since from lit - tle things a-round us, Great-er ones pro - ceed,

Lit - tle tho'ts, tho' soft-ly whispered, Heard in heav'n may be.
Bear it up - ward till its ech - oes Reach the heav'nly throng.
Let us try and live to Je - sus Ver - y near in - deed.

CHORUS.

Lit - tle hands were made to la - bor, Lit - tle hearts to pray,

Lit - tle feet to fol - low Je - sus, In the pleasant way.

JESUS, SAVIOUR, SON OF GOD.

ANON.   F. A. G. OUSELEY.

1. Je - sus, Saviour, Son of God, Who for me life's pathway trod,
2. I Thy lit - tle Lamb would be, Je - sus, I would fol-low Thee;
3. Teach me how to pray to Thee, Make me ho - ly, heaven - ly;

Who for me be-came a child, Make me humble, meek and mild.
Samuel was Thy child of old Take me, too, with - in Thy fold.
Let me love what Thou dost love, Let me live with Thee a - bove.

34 THE FIRST COMMANDMENT.

Mrs. J. C. F.

W. H. Doane.

1. Fa - ther, lead Thy little children Ve - ry ear-ly to Thy throne;
2. In the Bi-ble Thou hast taught us, All our tho'ts to Thee are known;
3. Though the heathen bow to idols They have made of wood and stone,
4. Thou dost give us all our comforts, Everything we call our own

ritard.

We will have no gods be-fore Thee; Thou art God, and Thou alone.
Thou canst see us in the darkness; Thou art God, and Thou alone.
We have Christian friends to tell us Thou art God, and Thou alone.
Comes from Thee, our heavenly Father; Thou art God, and Thou alone.

Lead, O lead Thy lit-tle children Ver - y ear-ly to Thy throne;

We will have no gods be-fore Thee; Thou art God, and Thou alone.

GOD CAN SEE ME EVERY DAY.

ANON.

HUBERT P. MAIN.

1. God can see me eve - ry day, When I work and when I play,
2. When I'm quiet, when I'm rude, When I'm naughty, when I'm good;
3. When the sun gives heat and light, When the stars do twinkle bright;

When I read and when I talk, When I run and when I walk,
When I'm hap - py, when I'm sad, When I'm sor - ry, when I'm glad;
When the moon shines on my bed, God still watches o'er my head;

When I eat and when I drink, When I sit and on - ly think,
When I pluck the scented rose That in my neat gar-den grows;
Night or day, at church or school, Learning how my life to rule,

When I laugh and when I cry, God is ev - er watching nigh.
When I crush the ti - ny fly, God is watching from on high.
God is marking all I say, Point - ing to the hap - py way.

PRETTY MOTH.

ANON.   ANON.

1. Fly a - way pretty moth to your home, On the
2. I have seen ma-ny ones in this world, Like your-

leaf where you've slumbered all day. Be con-tent with the
self, quite as bright and as gay, Who, bewitched by the

moon and the stars pret-ty moth, Now make use of your
sweet fas-cin - a - tions of life, Fluttered round them by

wings while you may. Tho' yon glit-ter-ing light May dazzle you
night and by day. But those dreams of delight Have dazzled them

quite, And the gold on you lamp may be gay, Ma - ny
quite, And the gold on you lamp may be gay, Ma - ny

things in this world that look bright, pretty moth, On - ly daz-zle to
things, &c.

lead us a - stray, Ma-ny things in this world that look

bright, pretty moth, On - ly daz - zle to lead us a - stray.

38 THE LITTLE MISSIONARY.

J. R. M.

1. I need not go to In - di - a, To Chi - na, or Ja - pan,
2. The lit - tle water-drops come down To make the flow-ers grow,
3. I'll be a Mis - sion-a - ry now, And work the best I may,

To work for Je - sus here at home. I'll do the best I can;
The lit - tle riv - u - lets flow on To bless where'er they go;
For if I *want* to work for God, There surely is a way;

I'll tell of His great love for me, And how I love Him too,
The lit-tle seeds make mighty trees, To cool us with their shade,
I'll pray for those who cross the sea, My offer-ing too, I'll send,

And bet - ter far, I'll show my love In all that I may do.
If lit - tle things like these do good, To try, *I'm* not a - fraid.
And do all that is in *my* power, This great, bad world, to mend

Copyright, 1883, by John Church & Co.

CHORUS.

We all may work for Je - sus, Where-ev - er we may be,

I'll try to work for Je - sus Who did so much for me.

- *DEAR JESUS, EVER AT MY SIDE.* *Tune, page 38.*

1 Dear Jesus, ever at my side,
How loving must Thou be
To leave Thy home in heaven, to
guard
A little child like me;
Thy beautiful and shining face
I see not, though so near;
The sweetness of Thy soft, low
voice,
I am too deaf to hear.

2 I cannot feel Thee touch my
hand
With pressure light and mild,
To check me as my mother did.
When I was but a child;

But I have felt Thee in my tho'ts
Fighting with sin for me;
And when my heart loves God, I
know
The sweetness is from Thee.

3 And when, dear Saviour! I kneel
down,
Morning and night to prayer,
Something, there is, within my
heart
Which tells me Thou art there;
Yes! when I pray, Thou prayest too—
Thy prayer is all for me;
But when I sleep, Thou sleepest not,
But watchest patiently.

Rev. F. W. Faber.

GOD ENTRUSTS TO ALL.

T. C. O'KANE, by per.

1. God en-trusts to all   Tal - ents few or ma - ny;
2. Tho' the great and wise   Have a great-er num-ber
3. God will sure-ly ask   Ere I en - ter hea - ven,

None so young and small   That they have not a - ny.
Yet my one I prize,   And it must not slumber.
Have I done the task   Which to me is giv - en.

CHORUS.

Tho' on-ly one, Tho' on-ly one   Un-to me be giv - en,

This I must use, this I must use, If I'd en-ter heaven.

TAKE ME, O MY SAVIOUR.

41

C. J. F.

B. C. Unseld.

1. Je - sus Thou canst make me Gen-tle as a lamb,
2. In life's hap - py spring-time Would I come to Thee,
3. Saviour may I nev - er From Thy love de-part,

Take me, O my Sav - iour, Take me as I am.
Let Thy ho - ly spir - it, Whisper now to me.
Be Thou al - ways near me, Dwell within my heart.

Chorus.

Teach my heart to love Thee, Teach my tongue to sing,

Thou art my Re - deem - er, Thou my gracious King.

COME LEARN OF THE WAY.

J. R. M.

J. R. Murray, by per.

1. Come learn of the way to the Saviour, He
2. To follow and find Him, the Saviour, We've
3. We must be good, and do good and love good, Each

bids us to come, you know; He wants all the
on - ly to do His sweet will; Be gen - tle and
sec - ond and min-ute and hour; Love each oth - er as

dear lit - tle children In His bless-ed foot-steps to go;
of good be - haviour, His ev - ery commandment ful - fill;
He has com-manded, And love God with all our power;

We need not to fight like the sol-diers, We need not to
Kind words and kind deeds bring Him near us, But bad ones will
Yes, be good, and do good, and love good. And love Him, and

toil like the men; We need not to go on a
drive Him a - way; So, what must we do, lit - tle
leave all the rest To Je - sus, who loves lit - tle

jour-ney, To find the dear Sav-iour a - gain.
chil-dren, To have Him with each of us stay.
chil-dren, And will do for them what is best.

LORD, ABIDE WITH ME.

F. J. C. SYLVESTER MAIN, by per.

1. Je - sus, Saviour! hear my call, Sin-ful tho' my heart may be,
2. Lone-ly in a stranger land, Cast me not a - way from Thee,
3. Fill me with Thy love di-vine, Con-se-crate my life to Thee,

Thou, my life, my hope, my all;—Lord, a - bide with me.
Lead me by Thy gen-tle hand;—Lord, a - bide with me.
Bend my stubborn will to Thine;—Lord, a - bide with me.

44 COME, LEARN OF THE MEEK AND LOWLY.

GRACE J. FRANCES.　　　　　　　　　　　　HUBERT P. MAIN.

1. Come, learn of the Meek and Low - ly, Come, sit at the
2. O if we were more like Je - sus, And more from the

REF. Come, learn of the Meek and Low - ly, Come, sit at the

Master's feet; No place in the world so ho - ly, No place in the
world a-part, Com-muning with Him in spir-it, And near-er to

Master's feet; No place in the world so ho - ly, No place in the

FINE.

world so sweet, His lessons are plain and simple, A balm to the
Him in heart,— We should not complain so sadly, When trouble and

world so sweet.

wounded breast; He mak-eth our bur - den light - er, And
care we meet, But car - ry at once our sor - rows, And

COME, LEARN OF THE MEEK.—Concluded. 45

D.C. for Refrain.

give-th His children rest.
lay them at Je - sus' feet.

3 He wept o'er the holy city,
  He wept o'er a loved one dead;
He knoweth our every trial,
  And seeth the tears we shed;
O live that our souls may enter
  His Kingdom with joy complete:
And there, through eternal ages,.
  We'll sit at the Master's feet.

F. T. PALGRAVE. ## MY SAVIOUR DEAR. T. E. PERKINS, by per.

1. Thou that once on mother's knee Wert a lit-tle one like me,
2. Be be - side me in the light, Close be-side me all the night,
3. Thou art near me when I pray, Tho' Thou art so far a - way;

When I wake or go to bed, Lay Thy hand a - bout my head;
Make me gen-tle, kind, and true, Do what mother bids me do.
Thou my lit - tle hymn wilt hear, Je - sus Christ, my Saviour dear.

Let me feel Thee ve - ry near, Je - sus Christ, my Saviour dear.
Help and cheer me when I fret, And for-give when I for-get.
Thou that once on mother's knee, Wert a lit - tle child like me.

46   JESUS, HIGH IN GLORY.

ANON.

W. LUDDEN, by per.

1. Je - sus, high in glo - ry, Lend a listening ear;
2. Save us, Lord, from sin - ning, Watch us day by day;

When we bow be - fore Thee, Children's prais - es hear;
Help us now to love Thee, Take our sins a - way;

Tho' Thou art so ho - ly, Heav'ns Al - might-y King,
Then when Je - sus calls us To our heavenly home,

Thou wilt deign to lis - ten When Thy praise we sing.
We would glad - ly an - swer, "Sav - iour, Lord, we come."

Mary L. Duncan.   H. R. Palmer.

Slowly, and with feeling.

1. Je-sus, tender Shepherd, hear me, Bless Thy little lamb to-night;
2. May my sins be all for-giv - en, Bless the friends I love so well;

Thro' the darkness be Thou near me, Keep me safe till morning light.
Take me, when I die, to heaven, Happy there with Thee to dwell.

All this day Thy hand has led me, And I thank Thee for Thy care,
Je - sus, tender Shepherd hear me, Bless Thy lit-tle lamb to-night;

Thou hast cloth'd me, warm'd me, fed me; Listen to my evening prayer.
Through the darkness be Thou near me, Keep me safe till morning light.

48　　　　　　HOSANNA!

FANNY J. CROSBY.　　　　　　　　　　　　　THEO. F. SEWARD.

1. Ho - san-na　in　the high-est!　In　Sa - lem's temple fair,
2. Ho - san-na　in　the high-est!　With joyful hearts we sing,
3. Ho - san-na　in　the high-est!　Be - hold! He pass-eth by,

The children sang to - geth - er, They knew the Lord was there.
We hail the Lord's A - noint - ed, Our great and Roy - al King;
With shouts let earth a - dore Him, And ev - ery creature cry:

And mul - ti-tudes who gathered On　that tri-umph-al　day,
'Tis finished! now, t'is　finished! The　mighty work is　done,
Ho - san - na　in　the　high-est! We　mag-ni - fy His name,

Cut down the palm-tree branches, And strew'd them in the　way.
And we may find　sal - va - tion Thro' Christ our Father's Son.
Ho - san-na　in　the　high-est! O sweet the loud ac-claim.

Chorus.—Teachers.

O list, as the children sing, How sweetly their voices ring!

Children.   **All.**

Ho - san - na in the high-est! Re - joice! the Lord is King!

JESUS, HOLY, UNDEFILED.

Mrs. E. SHEPCOTE.   J. B. DYKES.

1. Je - sus, Ho - ly, un - de-filed, Lis - ten to a lit - tle child:
2. Thou hast sent the sun to shine O'er this glorious world of Thine,
3. Now the lit - tle birds a - rise, Chirping gai - ly in the skies;
4. Thou, by whom the birds are fed, Give to me my dai - ly bread;

Thou hast sent the glorious light, Chasing far the si - lent night.
Warmth to give, and pleasant glow, On each ten-der flow'r be - low.
Thee their ti - ny voic - es praise, In the ear - ly songs they raise.
And Thy Ho - ly Spir - it give, Without whom I can-not live.

50 RAINDROPS, BIRDS AND FLOWERS.

J. R. M.   J. R. Murray, by per.

ONE VOICE.

1. Raindrops! Raindrops! Gent-ly   fall - ing from the   sky,
2. Flow-'rets! Flow-'rets! Does the   Lord have need of   you?

Tell   me, tell   me,   Why you leave your home   on high!
Tell   me, tell   me,   What is   there that   you   can do?

SEVERAL VOICES.

We   come   to make the grasses grow; We   come to   make the
We   come   to cheer the heart of man; We   come to   do   the

flow-ers   blow, We come because He   wills it   so,   Our
best we   can, We are   a   part of   His   great plan, Our

Motion Song—see page 4.

Fa - ther in the heav'ns. We love to do His
Fa - ther in the heav'ns.

bless - ed will, We'll try to fail Him nev - er, We

love His wish-es to ful - fil, For-ev - er and for-ev - er.

3 Birdies! Birdies!
Full of life and full of glee;
Tell me, tell me,
Why you sing so cheerily?
We sing because the skies are blue;
We sing because our hearts are true;
We sing because He wants us to,
Our Father in the heavens.

52 LITTLE ONES LIKE ME.

ANON.   JNO. R. SWENEY, by per.

1. Je - sus, when He left the sky, And for sinners came to
2. Mothers then the Saviour sought In the pla - ces where He
3. Did the Sav - iour say them nay? No, He kindly bade them
4. 'Twas for them His life He gave, To re - deem them from the

die, In His mer - cy passed not by Little ones like me.
taught, And to Him their children brought,—Little ones like me.
stay, Suffered none to turn a - way,—Little ones like me.
grave, Je - sus now will glad - ly save Little ones like me.

CHORUS.

Lit - tle ones, lit - tle ones, "Suffer them to come," said

Little ones, little ones,

He; Je - sus loves the lit - tle ones, Lit - tle ones like me.

MOTION SONG—See page 4. Copyright, 1880. by John J. Hood

MANSIONS ARE PREPARED ABOVE.

ANON.   HUBERT P. MAIN.

1. Mansions are prepared a - bove, By the gracious God of love;
2. Crowns that daz-zle hu - man eye, Wait for those who reach the sky;
3. Robes of spotless white are giv'n, By the glorious King of heav'n;
4. Harps of joy-ful sound a - bove, Swell the praise of Je-sus' love;

Ma - ny will those mansions see—Is there one pre-pared for me?
Ma - ny there those crowns will see, Is there one pre-pared for me?
All can have them, they are free,—Is there one pre-pared for me?
Oh! how sweet their strains will be,—Is there, Lord, a harp for me?

CHORUS.

Is there one for me? Is there one for me? Ma - ny

will those mansions see, Is there one pre-pared for me?

MOTION SONG—See page 4.

54   GOD HAS MADE ALL THINGS.

Mrs. C. F. Alexander.   Geo. C. Stebbins.

1.   All things bright and beautiful, All creatures great and small,
2. Each lit - tle flow'r that o - pens, Each little bird that sings,
3. The pur - ple head-ed moun-tain, The riv - er running by,
4. He gave us eyes to see them, And lips that we might tell,

All things wise and wonderful, The Lord has made them all.
He made their glowing col - ors, He made their ti - ny wings.
The sun - set and the morn-ing That brightens up the sky.
How great is God Al - might-y, Who has made all things well.

:S: Chorus.

"In the be - gin-ning God cre - a - ted the heaven and the

D S.—In the be - gin - ning, God cre - a - ted the heav - en and the

FINE.   D S.

earth," The heaven and the earth, The heaven and the earth.

earth.   Copyright,1883, by Biglow & Main.

Motion Song—See page 4.

Rev. Paxton Hood.   J. C. Engelbrecht arr.

1. There's a beautiful land where the rains never beat, And the cold winds never blow, And they feel not the glow of the summer heat, Nor the chill of the win-ter snow, Nor the chill of the win-ter snow.

2 There is many a child in that beautiful land;
   We've brothers and sisters there;
   And they dwell with the angels—a happy band—
   Their glory and joy to share.

3 And they never die in that beautiful land,
   And the people are always young;
   And their cheeks with the roses of health are fanned,
   And their voices are always in song.

4 And Jesus lives in that beautiful land,
   And He says to the children "Come;"
   And sometimes He takes them from our band,
   To dwell in that beautiful home.

56 FOLLOW ME.

C. J. F.

B. Carl Unseld.

1. Je - sus, if Thy child should stray, Heedless from Thy side away,
2. Should this wayward heart of mine Round some earthly pleasure twine,

Let me hear Thee kind-ly say, "Fol - low Me." If my feet should
Speak a-gain those words divine, "Fol - low Me." Tho' bereft of

wea - ry grow, In the way Thou bid'st me go, Take my hand and
all most dear, On - ly Thee my soul to cheer, Let me still Thy

Chorus.

whis-per low, "Fol - low Me." Fol-low Me, fol - low Me,
ac-cents hear, "Fol - low Me."

Never doubting, follow Me.

3 Thro' the furnace tho' I tread,
If by Thee my steps are led.
I will go, for Thou hast said
　"Follow Me."
When I reach the swelling tide,
Thou the waters wilt divide,
Thou wilt whisper by my side—
　"Follow Me."

JESUS, LEAD MY HEART TO THEE.

FANNY J. CROSBY.　　　　　　　　W. F. SHERWIN.

1. Je - sus, lead my heart to Thee; Help my weak en -
2. I would love Thee eve - ry day, I would grieve Thee
3. Hast Thou borne the cross for me? Then, with - out re -

deav - or Still Thy faithful child to be; Lov - ing Sav - iour,
nev - er; Saviour, teach me how to pray, Keep me in the
pin - ing, Let me bear it now for Thee; Cheer-ful, Lord, what-

ritard.

dwell with me, Make me Thine for - ev - er.
nar - row way, Make me Thine for - ev - er.
e'er it be, All to Thee re - sign - ing.

Copyrighted, 1869, in "Bright Jewels."

HERE AND THERE.

Miss Lucy J. Rider, by per.

1. Day by day, the glorious sun   Rises clear and bright.
2. Every spring the sweet young flowers   Blossom bright and gay,
3. Little birds sing songs of praise   All the summer long,

But the evening cometh on,   And   the | cold   dark | night.
But the chilling autumn hours With - er | them   a - | way.
But in colder, shorter, days, They   for-| get   their | song.

REFRAIN.—*Joyfully.*

There is a bright land far away, Where 'tis nev-er ending day;
There is a land we have not seen, Where the fields are always green;
There is a place where angels sing Cease-less prais-es to their King;

There is a bright land far away, Where 'tis nev-er ending day.
There is a land we have not seen, Where the fields are always green.
There is a place where angels sing Ceaseless prais-es to their King.

4 Who shall go to that bright land? |
All who love the Lord; |
All who follow His command,
All who | keep His | Word.
Ref.—Children, come and join the band
Marching to that happy land.

GUARD, MY CHILD, THY TONGUE.

Anon.   H. R. PALMER, by per.

1. Guard, my child, thy tongue, That it speaks no wrong: Let no e - vil
2. Guard, my child, thine eyes; Pry-ing is not wise: Let them look on
3. Guard, my child, thine ear; Wicked words will sear; Let no e - vil

word pass o'er it; Set the watch of truth be-fore it, That it do no
what is right; From all e - vil turn thy sight; Pry-ing is not
word come in, That may cause the soul to sin, Wicked words will

wrong, Guard, my child, thy tongue.
wise, Guard, my child, thine eyes.
sear, Guard, my child, thine ear.

4.
Ear, and eye, and tongue,
Guard while thou art young;
For, alas! these busy three,
Can unruly members be,
Guard, while thou art young,
Ears, and eyes, and tongue.

MOTION SONG—See page 4.

JESUS IN THE MANGER.

R. S. C.

Mrs. T. J. Cook.

1. What do we find in the man-ger, On this sa - cred morn?

Lo! a precious stranger, Je - sus Christ is born! Glo-ry,

glo-ry be to God on high! Glo-ry, glo-ry be to God on high!

2 Bethlehem of Judea
   Is the chosen place,
Where the Infant Treasure
   Comes to bless our race.

| 3 Shepherds, with fear and trem-
   Hear an Angel voice   [bling,
Bearing gladsome tidings,
   Bidding them rejoice.

4 Spices and costly tribute,
   Choicest gifts of gold,
Are, in free oblation,
   Brought by men of old.

5 We will give adoration,
   Hearts of fervent love,
Telling every nation,
   Jesus reigns above!

LEAD ME EVERY DAY.

FANNY J. CROSBY.

W. H. DOANE.

61

1. Je - sus, Thou art call-ing me . Eve - ry day, eve - ry day;
2. Keep me ver - y close to Thee Eve - ry day, eve - ry day;
3. I would love Thee more and more Eve - ry day, eve - ry day;
4. Teach me les-sons pure and sweet Eve - ry day, eve - ry day;

Thou dost bid me fol - low Thee, I am com-ing right a - way.
Ver - y hum-ble may I be, Ver-y earnest when I pray.
Thinking all Thy mer-cy o'er, When I work and when I pray.
Thou canst make my willing feet Strong to run the heavenly way.

REFRAIN.

Help, O help me, Saviour mine, Lest I wan-der from the way;

Hold my lit - tle hand in Thine, Lead me eve - ry day.

WORDS OF JESUS.

J. R. MURRAY, by per.

CHANT.

AND JESUS SAID:
1. Suffer little children to come unto me, and for-
2. I am the
3. This is my commandment that ye

bid them not, For of such is the
Good Shepherd; My sheep hear my voice, and I know them, and they
love one another; Ye are my friends if ye do whatsoever

SEMI-CHORUS. *Little Children.*

king - dom of heaven.   We come, O blessed Sav - iour, We
fol - low   Me.   We fol - low, blessed Sav - iour, Thy
I   command you.   Help us, O blessed Sav - iour, Thy

hear Thy gen-tle voice;   We come to do Thy bid-ding, And
lit - tle lambs are we;   O keep our feet from straying, Till
lit - tle friends to be;   And in our love for others, Show

FULL CHORUS.

in Thy love re-joice. We come, we come, We hear Thy welcome
we Thy face shall see.
best our love for Thee.

we come, we come,

call; Thy great, warm, loving heart has room For the little ones and all.

THE CHILD'S GIFT TO GOD.

ANON.   HUBERT P. MAIN.

1. Two lit-tle eyes to look to God. Two little ears to hear His word;
2. One little tongue to speak His truth, One little heart for Him, in youth;

Two lit-tle feet to walk His ways, Hands to serve Him all my days.
Take them, oh Je-sus, let them be, Always will-ing, true to Thee.

MOTION SONG—See page 4. Copyright, 1883, by Biglow & Main

64 EASTER CAROL.

MARY A. LATHBURY.   MRS. MARY C. SEWARD.

1. Lift up, O lit-tle chil-dren, Your voi-ces clear and sweet,
2. Lift up, O ten-der lil-ies, Your whiteness to the sun;
3. Ring, all ye bells of Eas-ter, Your chimes of joy a-gain,

And sing the blessed sto-ry Of Christ, the Lord of glo-ry,
The earth is not our pris-on, Since Christ Himself hath risen,
Ring out the night of sad-ness, Ring in the morn of gladness,

And worship at His feet, And worship at His feet.
The life of ev-'ry one, The life of ev-'ry one.
For death no more shall reign, For death no more shall reign.

CHORUS.

Oh, sing the blessed sto-ry! The Lord of life and glo-ry

Is ris-en, as He said, Is ris-en from the dead!

NOAH'S DOVE.

W. F. SHERWIN.

1. Dear lit - tle Dove, when I think of you, I wish I may
2. Dear lit - tle Dove, O you did not know Who sheltered and
3. Dear lit - tle Dove, how you trust - ed one Who kept you all

flee for safe - ty too; A storm is com - ing, when the
kept you, and loved you so; But I am learn-ing how the
safe till the storm was done; May I trust Je - sus and be

Lord will be To those who love Him, like the Ark to thee.
Son of God, To save my soul, once shed His precious blood.
sheltered too; There's an Ark for me, as well as one for you.

66 WHAT GOD GIVES.

ANON.   THEO. F. SEWARD.

1. God cares for ev - ery lit - tle child That on this large earth
2. He gives them all their lov-ing friends, He gives each child its
3. He makes the earth all beau-ti - ful, He makes thine eyes to
4. What can a lit - tle child give? From His bright heav'n a-

liv - eth; He gives them home and food and clothes, And
moth - er, He gives them all the hap - pi - ness Of
see And touch and hear-ing, taste and smell, He
bove, The great God smiles and reach - es down To

CHORUS.

more than these God giv - eth.   For He is al - ways
lov - ing one an - oth - er.
gives them all to Thee.
take His children's love.

giv - ing To eve - ry creature liv - ing; How can we love and praise e - nough The God who's ev - er giv - ing!

CHILDREN'S THANKS.

FANNY J. CROSBY. W. F. SHERWIN, by per.

1. With gladsome hearts our praise we bring To God who is the
2. For all the sweetness of that grace Which gives the lit-tle

children's King, Who bends to list - en when they sing; For
ones a place Where they may see the Saviour's face; For

this we thank Thee, Lord.
this we thank Thee, Lord.

3.
We thank Thee for this holy day,
When we may read Thy word and
pray,
And learn to walk in wisdom's way;
For this we thank Thee, Lord.

MOTION SONG—See page 4.

THE BIRDS AND THE BOTTLE.

(A flock of birds found, one day, in the woods, a bottle of strong drink that some poor drunkard had dropped, and while they were wondering about it, this is what one of the wise ones said:)

J. R. M.   J. R. MURRAY, by per.

1. "Bob-o-link, do not drink," Said a hap-py lit-tle
2. "Tweet, tweet, tweet, little feet, Go not near it, I re-

bird,   Swinging   on   the   branches   high;
peat, It will fill your   lit-tle   heart with   pain;

"Pee-wee-wee, let   it   be, 'Tis not good for you   or
Run, run, run, shun it, shun, It   is   worse than an-y

me, If   you touch it   you   will   sure-ly   die.
gun; If   you drink you'll nev-er   sing   a-gain.

Pure cold wa - ter is the drink, We do tru - ly, tru - ly

think, For all the liv - ing things that God has made;

So birds, and boys, and men, We re - peat a - gain, a -

gain, To sing its praise must nev - er be a - fraid.

70 NOW I LAY ME DOWN TO SLEEP.

FANNY J. CROSBY.

THOS. J. COOK.

1. In the west the beams of day Slow - ly, soft - ly,
2. Je - sus, hear my sim - ple pray'r, Take me now be -

die a - way: Now the eve - ning shadows fall - ing,
neath Thy care,— Thou whose gen-tle hand has led me

All my bet - ter tho'ts re - call - ing, Wrap the earth in
All day long, and kind - ly fed me, Still Thy child in

si - lence deep; Now I lay me down to sleep.
safe - ty keep, While I lay me down to sleep.

SAVIOUR, GENTLE SAVIOUR. ✗ 71

Mrs. Ruth Harmon.   Rev. Samuel Alman.

1. May we all Thy children be, Saviour, gen-tle Saviour;
2. Children once by Thee were blessed, Saviour, gen-tle Saviour;
3. We may now Thy bless-ing share, Saviour, gen-tle Saviour;
4. Teach me still Thy name to love, Saviour, gen-tle Saviour;

Keep us ver - y near to Thee, Saviour, gen-tle Sav - iour.
In Thine arms, how sweet their rest, Saviour, gen-tle Sav - iour.
Thou wilt hear our sim-ple prayer, Saviour, gen-tle Sav - iour.
Fix our thoughts on things a - bove, Saviour, gen-tle Sav - iour.

Chorus.

Lead, O lead us ev - ery day, Saviour, gen - tle Sav-iour;

Then from Thee we will not stray, Saviour, gen-tle Sav - iour.

72   CHILDREN, COME.

C. J. F.   Wm. B. Bradbury.

CHO.-1. Lift a - loud your songs of praise, Children, come, children, come;
2. God in - v'tes you in His word, Children, come, children, come;
3. Hear the Sav-iour gent-ly call, Children, come, children, come;

Up to God your voic-es raise, Children, children, come;
Oft you have His bidding heard, Children, children, come;
I've a wel-come for you all, Children, children, come;

Semi-chorus or Quartet.

He can hear each little voice, He can make each heart rejoice,
Come, and choose the narrow way, Come, nor from my precepts stray,
Come, and share my tender love, Come, my promised kindness prove,

ALL.   D.C. *for Chorus.*

He can give you blessings choice, Children, come, O come.
Come, prepare for end-less day, Children, come, O come.
Come, and learn of heav'n a-bove, Children, come, O come.

     Come, O come, yes.

MAKE US PATIENT.

MARY A. LATHBURY.   HUBERT P. MAIN.

1. Ev - ery lil - y in the meadow Waits in patience for the rain;
2. Blessed Saviour, it is written, "Be ye patient" in Thy word;

Ev - ery dai - sy in the shadow, Waits till sunshine comes again;
Make us patient as the lil - y, Or the dai - sy, or the bird;

Ev - ery bird-ie in the home nest, Waits for food, nor waits in vain,
Give us hearts like Thine, dear Jesus, Ne-ver by impatience stirred;

Ev - ery bird-ie in the home nest, Waits for food, nor waits in vain.
Give us hearts like Thine, dear Jesus, Never by impatience stirred.

74   STAR, BEAUTIFUL STAR.

R. W. RAYMOND.   FRED. SCHILLING, 1868, by per.

1. There's a beau-ti - ful star, a beau-ti - ful star, The
2. In the land of the East, in the shadows of night, We
3. We have gold for trib-ute and gifts for prayer. In -

wea - ry trav'lers have followed far, Shining so bright-ly
saw the glo-ry of thy new light, Tell - ing us, in our
cense and myrrh, and spi - ces rare: All that we have, we

all the way, Till it stood o'er the place where the young child lay.
distant home. The King - Re-deem-er to earth had come!
hither bring, To lay it with joy at feet of the King.

CHORUS.

Star, star, beau-ti - ful star! Pilgrims wea-ry we are; To

Je - sus, to Je - sus, We fol-low thee from a - far.

DAY BY DAY.

Rev. JOHN ELLERTON.   J. B. DYKES, Mus. Doc.

1. Day   by day we magnify Thee—When our hymns in school we raise;
2. Day   by day   we   mag - ni-fy Thee—Not in words of praise alone;
3. Day   by day   we   mag - ni-fy Thee, When, for Jesus' sake we try

Dai - ly work be-gun and end - ed With the dai-ly voice of praise.
Truthful lips and meek o-be-dience Show Thy glory in Thine own.
Every wrong to bear with patience, Eve - ry sin to mor-ti - fy.

4 Day by day we magnify Thee,
    Till our days on earth shall cease;
    Till we rest from these our labors,
    Waiting for Thy day in peace.

5 Then, on that eternal morning
    With Thy great redeemed host,
    May we fully magnify Thee
    Father, Son, and Holy Ghost!

76 THERE'S A FRIEND FOR LITTLE CHILDREN.

ALBERT MIDLANE.   SAMUEL SMITH.

1. There's a Friend for lit-tle children A-bove the bright blue sky,
2. There's a home for lit-tle children A-bove the bright blue sky,
3. There's a song for lit-tle children A-bove the bright blue sky,

A Friend that nev-er changes, Whose love will nev-er die.
Where Je-sus reigns in glo - ry, A home of peace and joy.
And harps of sweetest mu-sic, And palms of vic - to - ry:

Un - like our friends by nature, Who change with changing years;
No home on earth is like it, Nor can with it compare.
And all a - bove is pleasure, And found in Christ a - lone:

This Friend is al - ways worthy The precious name He bears.
For eve - ry one is hap - py, Nor can be happier there.
Oh, come, dear lit-tle child-ren, That all may be your own.

F. J. C.

Mrs. J. F. KNAPP, by per.

1. We are children, happy children, Singing, singing as we go;
2. Do not let the joys around us Tempt our little feet to stray,
3. If we try to fol-low Je - sus, Try to serve Him here below,

'Tis our Father's hand that leads us, Leads us thro' this world below.
O our Father, kind-ly keep us In the strait and narrow way.
Where He lives and dwells for-ev-er, Singing, singing shall we go.

CHORUS.

Glo-ry, glo-ry, let us sing, Glo-ry, glo-ry, let us sing,

Praise to God, praise to God, Praise to God our heavenly King.

78   JESUS, SAVIOUR, LOOK UPON US.

F J. C.

THEO. F. SEWARD.

1. Je - sus, Saviour, look up - on us, In our Sab - bath
2. Grant that not our voic - es on - ly Join our ope - ning
3. When the fer - vent prayer is offered, May we all at

home to - day; May Thy bless - ed, Ho - ly Spir - it
hymn to sing; But from souls with rapture glow-ing,
ten - tive be; Look - ing up with true de - vo - tion.

CHORUS.

Turn our tho'ts from earth a - way. Come, O come, di - vine In -
May Thy praise re-spon-sive ring.
Look - ing up by faith to Thee.

structor, Teach us wisdom from a - bove; Touch these youthful hearts be - fore Thee, Melt them each and all to love.

4 When to us Thy word unfolded,
   Tells how just and good Thou art;
   May it drop, and live, and sparkle
   Like a gem in every heart.

5 Saviour hear us, guide and keep us,
   Make us useful here below;
   Then at last in heaven receive us,
   Where immortal pleasures flow.

THE CHILDREN'S CREED.

Rev. W. F. CRAFTS.   E. H. C., by per.

1. Je - sus, Saviour, Thee I love   For Thy dy-ing love to me;
2. Trusting Thee, my Saviour true, All my sins to take a-way;
3. "Seek me car-ly" I have heard. And my heart is answering "Yes;"

Send the Ho - ly Spir - it dove Ev - er in my heart to be.
Sin - ful things I'll cease to do; Fol - low Je - sus eve - ry day.
Listening ear-ly to Thy Word, All my days are hap-pi-ness.

80 IF YOU HAVE A PLEASANT THOUGHT.

Rob. Morris, L.L.D.   H. R. Palmer, by per.

1. If you have a pleasant tho't, Sing it,   sing it;
2. Eve-ry gracious deed of His, Sing it,   sing it;
3. Are you wea-ry, are you sad— Sing it,   sing it;

As   the birds sing in their sport, Sing it from the heart;
Noth-ing sounds so   well as   this, Sing it from the heart;
Make yourselves and oth-ers glad, Sing it from the heart;

Does the Ho - ly Spir - it move, For the children of His love—
How the Lord walk'd on the wave, Rescued Lazarus from the grave,
Bless-ed ones be - fore His face, Sing of Christ's a-toning grace,

Sing, and point the home a - bove, Sing it from the heart.
Died our guilt-y souls to save, Sing it from the heart.
Give the Saviour end - less praise, Sing it from the heart.

CHORUS.

Singing, singing from the heart, O, the joy our songs im-part!

Je - sus, bless the tune-ful art, Singing from the heart.

SAVIOUR, WHO THY FLOCK.

Rev. W. A. MUHLENBERG.   Rev. EDMUND S. CARTER.

1. Saviour! who Thy flock art feeding With the Shepherd's kindest care,
2. Nev - er from Thy pas-ture roving, Let them be the li-on's prey;
3. Then, with-in Thy fold e - ter - nal, Let them find a resting-place,

All the fee - ble gen-tly leading.While the lambs Thy bosom share.
Let Thy ten-der-ness, so loving,Keep them all life's dangerous way.
Feed in pastures ev - er ver-nal, Drink the rivers of Thy grace.

MOTION SONG—See page 5.

Rev. W. F. CRAFTS. J. R. MURRAY, by per.

1. A won-der - ful house have I, That God has made for me.
2. A fountain is in the house, A pitch-er lies at hand;
3. And when this house shall fall; As death at last shall come;

With windows to see the sky, And keepers strong and free.
And strong men God has giv - en, To bear me o'er the land.
The good have a bet - ter house A - bove, in Je - sus' home.

DUET.

The door has a tuneful harp, A mill to grind my bread,
The keepers must work for God; The harp must sing His praise;
Yes, when this house shall fall, As death at last shall come;
Organ.

ALL.

And there is a gold-en bowl, A beautiful sil - ver thread,
The windows look up to heaven; The strong men walk His ways.
The good have a bet - ter house A - bove, in Je-sus' home.

MOTION SONG—See page 5. Copyright, 1880, by John Church & Co

Rev. J. KING.   BERTHOLD TOURS.

1. When, His sal - va - tion bringing, To Zi - on Je - sus came,
2. And since the Lord re-tain - eth His love for children still,
3. For should we fail pro-claiming Our great Redeemer's praise,

The children all stood singing, Ho - san - na to His name;
Tho' now as king He reigneth On Zi - on's heav'nly hill;
The stones, our silence shaming, Would their ho-san-nas raise.

Nor did their zeal of - fend Him, But as He rode a - long,
We'll flock around His ban-ner, Who sits up - on the throne,
But shall we on - ly ren-der The tribute of our words?

He let them still at-tend Him, And listened to their song.
And cry a - loud, " Ho-san - na To Da - vid's roy - al Son."
No: while our hearts are tender, They, too, shall be the Lord's.

84 ONE ROSY CROWN OF LOVE.

GRACE J. FRANCES.

HUBERT P. MAIN.

1. They crowned our Saviour's brow with thorns, They pierced and
2. Our hands shall gath-er ros - es sweet For Him our
3. He trod for us a thorn-y path; He died for

made it bleed; And not con-tent they mocked Him then, And
Saviour King, And glad-ly in our Sab - bath home, We'll
you and me; Our love, the pur-est we can give, That

REFRAIN.

struck Him with a reed. Oh, what a kind, for - giv-ing
crown Him while we sing.
ros - y crown shall be.

Lord, Such cru - el pain to bear, That we who trust Him

as we ought, A crown of life might wear!

THE DOVE AND THE RAVEN.

MARY A. LATHBURY. Arr. by L. J. R.

1. Once a gen-tle snow white bir-die Came and built its nest,
2. Then how hap-py, gen-tle, lov-ing, Grew the ba - by Grace,

In a spot you'd nev-er dream of, In a ba - by's breast.
All the smiles and all the dim-ples Brightened in her face.

3 But a black and ugly raven
   Came one morn this way;
   Came, and drove the gentle birdie
   From its nest away.

4 Ah! how frowning and unlovely
   Was our Gracie then,
   Until evening brought the white dove
   To its nest again.

5 Children, this was Gracie's raven—
   This her gentle dove—
   In her heart a *naughty Temper*
   Drove away the *Love*.

MOTION SONG—See page 5.

86   IN THE TEMPLE SANG THE CHILDREN.

GRACE J. FRANCES.   HUBERT P. MAIN.

DUET.

1. In the tem-ple   sang the children   As the Sav - iour
2. Crowds ad-vancing closed a - round Him, And the noon-tide's
3. "Blessed be   the   Son   of Da - vid," Filled the air and

passed a - long; Sang "Ho - san - na   in the high-est,
gold - en   ray   Saw them scat - ter   palm-tree branches,
rent the   sky;   "Bless-ed   be   the   King who com-eth"

FULL CHORUS.

While the ea - ger, listening throng Caught the soul-in-spir - ing
With their garments, in His way.   Still the children sang "Ho-
In   the name of God most high;" Bless-ed   be our lov - ing

chor - us,   Of   the children's hap - py song, Caught the
san - na"   On   that great tri-umph-al   day,   Still the &c.
Sav - iour, Glad - ly now our hearts' re - ply,   Bless - ed. &c.

soul in - spir-ing chor-us Of the children's hap-py song.

EASTER SONG.

MARY A. LATHBURY.

L. L. B, by per.

1. Snow-drops! lift your timid heads, All the earth is waking, Field and
2. Lil - ies! lil - ies! Easter calls! Rise to meet the dawning Of the
3. Waken, sleeping but-ter-flies, Burst your narrow prison! Spread your

for - est, brown and dead. In - to life are wak-ing; Snow-drops,
bless - ed light that falls Thro' the Easter morn-ing; Ring your
gold - en wings and rise, For the Lord is ris - en; Spread your

rise. and tell the sto - ry, How He rose. the Lord of glo - ry.
bells and tell the sto - ry. How He rose, the Lord of glo - ry.
wings and tell the sto - ry. How He rose, the Lord of glo - ry.

MOTION SONG—see page 5.

A CHRISTMAS CAROL.

MARY A. LATHBURY. LUCY L. BEEDE, arr.

1. The an-gels, the an - gels, Who sang on a Christmas eve. And
2. "Glad tidings, glad tidings, To you, to you we bring, Of
3. The Saviour, the Saviour, Of whom the an-gels sang, Did

waked the shepherds so long a - go, What was the song that they
peace on earth, and good will to men!" And an-gels ech - oed the
all. the peo - ple go forth to meet, And pal - ace por - tals un -

carol - ed so? The an - gels, the an - gels Who
song a - gain, "Glad ti - dings, glad ti - dings, To
fold to greet The Sav - iour, the Sav - iour Of

sang on a Christmas eve.
you, to you we bring!"
whom the an - gels sang?

4 They found Him—they found Him
Beneath the Eastern Star,
And kings and shepherds kneeled
down to pray
Around the manger where Jesus
lay.
They found Him—they found Him
Beneath the Eastern Star.

AAAAAAAAA

A CHRISTMAS CAROL.—Concluded. 89

5 What treasure—what treasure
  Can little children bring?
  And where is the blessed Redeemer now
    That round His cradle we all may bow?
  What treasure—what treasure
  Can little children bring?

6 No treasure—no treasure
  Is half so sweet to Him
  As little children; greet Him here
    With loving heart and open ear.
  No treasure—no treasure
  Is half so sweet Him.

THE CHILD'S FIRST PRAYER.

ANON.   HUBERT P. MAIN.

Now I lay me down to sleep, I pray the Lord my soul to keep; If
I should die be-fore I wake, I pray the Lord my soul to take.

Copyright, 1883, by Biglow & Main.

IN THE MORNING.

Through the night with slumber pressed,
The Lord hath given me quiet rest;
Let mercy guide me through the day,
And lead me in the narrow way.

90   'T IS THE HOLY SPIRIT CALLING.

Fanny J. Crosby.   Rev. R. Lowry

1. Soft and low there comes a whisper; Many times we hear it say,
2. 'T is the Ho - ly Spir-it leads us To the feet of Christ the Lord;
3. 'T is the Ho - ly Spir-it shows us What our lives must always be.

"Je - sus loves and loves you dearly, Will you be His friend to-day?"
Making plain our ev-ery du - ty Thro' the teaching of His word;
If we hope, be-yond the riv - er, Face to face our Lord to see;

'T is the Ho - ly Spir-it call-ing; God the Father sent Him here.
'T is the same e - ter-nal Spir-it That, descending from a - bove,
When we pray to God the Father, Thro' His well be-lov - ed Son,

In the name of our Re-deem-er, All our steps to guide and cheer.
Came and rest-ed on the Saviour, Like a pure and gen-tle dove.
We must pray to God the Spir-it, For the blessed Three are One.

GRACE J. FRANCES.   HUBERT P. MAIN.

1. We're soldiers of an ar - my, A no - ble temp'rance band;
2. Our no - ble temp'rance ar-my Is press-ing on its way,
3. Tho' young.we know the Saviour Is ev - er near at hand, .

And in its cause u - nit - ed, We la - bor heart and hand;
We see its ranks increas-ing, And stronger ev - ery day;
To cheer us in our la - bor.And bless our growing band;

We're soldiers of an ar - my. For vol-un-teers we call,
And still there's room for oth-ers, We glad-ly welcome all.
And if we ask be - liev-ing, He'll give us each and all,

To fight our valiant he - roes. A-gainst King Al - co-hol.
Who come to join the bat-tle, A-gainst King Al - co-hol.
The strength we need for bat-tle, A-gainst King Al - co-hol.

TAKE MY HAND, DEAR JESUS.

KATE OSBORN.　　　　　　　　　　　　　　W. W. BENTLEY, by per.

With feeling.

1. Ev - er blessed Je - sus, List-en un - to me; Bow Thine
2. Ev - er blessed Je - sus, Bless thy wayward child, Keep my
3. Help me, blessed Je - sus, Leave me not a - lone; Give me

ear and hear me, While I call to Thee; I am weak and
feet from straying Thro' the des-ert wild; I would nev - er
strength and patience Till each du-ty's done; And when life is

sin - ful, Thou art pure and strong; Take my hand, dear Je - sus,
wan-der From Thy lov-ing side; Ev - er bless-ed Je - sus,
end-ed, I Thy face would see; Hear my pray'r dear Je-sus,

CHORUS.

Lead Thy child a - long. Take my hand, dear Je - sus, Let me
Be my constant Guide.
Take me up to Thee.

nev - er stray; Take my hand and lead me In the better way.

HOW CAN A CHILD BE SAVED?

ANON.

THEO. F. SEWARD.

1. 2. How can a child be saved, His sins be all for - given?

CHO—*So can a child be saved, His sins be all for - given;*

FINE.

How may He in his dy - ing day Stand at the gate of Heaven?

So may he in his dy - ing day Stand at the gate of Heaven.

D.C. *for Chorus.*

{ He must re-pent with all his heart, And strive to serve his God. }
{ In sim-ple faith he must re-ly On Christ's a-ton - ing blood. }
{ Thro' that a - lone is welcome found At yon-der pearl-y gate; }
{ Thousands have entered, young as we, Nor shall we lingering wait. }

94 I WILL PRAY.

Mrs. Helen E. Brown.

W. H. Doane.

1. I will pray, I will pray, Night and morning, ev - ery day;
2. I will pray, I will pray, "Je - sus help me to o - bey
3. I will pray, I will pray, When I'm sor - ry, when I'm gay;

D C.—*I will pray, &c.*

FINE.

Fold my hands, and lift my eyes To my Je - sus in the skies;
All Thy wise and ho - ly will; All Thy wish-es to ful-fill;
If my precious Saviour smile, I am hap - py all the while;

I will pray, I will pray. "Je - sus wash my guilt a - way;
I will pray, I will pray, At my work and at my play,
I will pray, I will pray, E - ven in my dy - ing day,—

D.C.

Make my spir-it pure with-in, Keep my soul from ev - ery sin."
All to help, and all to love, As the an - gels do a - bove.
" O'er the stream, so dark and wild, Je-sus, take Thy lit - tle child."

ALONE WITH JESUS.

Grace J. Frances.   Hubert P. Main.

1. When at morn we wake from sleep, Go a - lone with Je - sus;
2. When we feel our souls are weak, Go a - lone with Je - sus;
3. In   the lit - tle griefs we bear, Go a - lone with Je - sus;
4. Go   to Him what-e'er we need, Go a - lone with Je - sus;

Ask of Him our hearts to keep, Go a - lone with Je - sus.
He   will give the strength we seek, Go a - lone with Je - sus.
He   will lighten eve - ry care, Go a - lone with Je - sus.
Trust in Him, His promise plead, Go a - lone with Je - sus.

CHORUS.

Go to Him without de - lay, On - ly He can guide our way;

Don't for - get to watch and pray, Go a - lone with Je - sus.

96   LIKE MERRY BIRDS WE COME.

F. J. C.

Mrs. J. F. KNAPP, by per.

1. Like mer - ry birds we come; A   hap-py song we bring, Of
2. We wish our eyes had seen The ho - ly angel throng, Who
3. God made a bright, new star To crown that hap-py morn; How
4. And we, tho' young and small, Are thankful when we sing; Good

Christ our dear Re-deemer's birth We, children, too, can sing.
came to earth on wings of light, And filled the air with song.
glad the shepherds were to hear That Christ the Lord was born.
will and peace from heav'n to all, Thro' Christ our Saviour King.

pp CHORUS.   *f*   *pp*

Glo - ry to God, Glo - ry to God, Glo - ry to God,

f

Glo - ry to God, Glo - ry to God in the high - est!

Glo - ry to God in the high - - est!

ON THIS HAPPY BIRTH-DAY.

Mrs. CHARLOTTE B. MERRITT. Mrs. SARAH L. WARNER.

1. On this hap - py birth-day Of our Saviour King,
2. Bethle-hem's star is shin - ing, Ho - ly is its ray,
3. Now He reigns for - ev - er, Lov - ing you and me;

Come, dear lit - tle chil - dren, Sweet-ly let us sing.
To the world pro-claim-ing Christ was born to - day.
Joy - ful, let us praise Him Round our Christmas tree.

Of the Christ Child, Of the Christ Child, We will gladly sing.
Of the Christ Child, Of the Christ Child, We will gladly sing.
To the Christ Child, To the Christ Child, We our tribute bring.

98 LITTLE CHILDREN, YOU MAY COME.

Julia A. Mathews.   Rev. R. Lowry.

Gently.

1. Lit - tle chil-dren, press-ing near To the feet of
2. Nay, you know not Christ the King; He no cost - ly
3. Well we know that we are touched With the deep, dark

Christ the King. Have you nei - ther doubt nor fear?
gift de - mands; More than gold or sparkl-ing gems,
stain of sin; Well we know its shad - ow falls

Or, some trib - ute do you bring? Are your lit - tle
Je - sus loves our lit - tle hands; Empt-y though they
All a - round, without, with - in; But our Sav -

hands so filled With bright gold and rar-est gem, That you
be, and weak. He will take them in His own; He will
knows it too. And He bids us still to come; Trusting

dare to press so close Ev - en touch His garment's hem?
bend to hear our prayer, Ev - en from His gra-cious throne.
in His ten - der love, Press we fear-less toward His home.

CHORUS.

Lit - tle chil - dren, you may come to Him; If you

want Him you may come to Him, For He waits this

ver - y day, All your sins to take a - way.

4 He will cleanse our guilty stains;
   Give us robes so fair and white,
   That we shall not dread to stand
   E'en before God's piercing sight;

Holy angels cannot sing
   Such a joyous, gladsome song,
   As the happy little ones,
   Who to Christ the Lord belong.

100 RING, YE HAPPY CHRISTMAS BELLS.

Mrs. CHARLOTTE B. MERRITT.   H. P. DANKS.

Sprightly.

1. Ring, ye hap-py Christmas bells, Ring the precious sto - ry:
2. Lit - tle children, come and learn, Learn the sweet old sto - ry;
3. Stars and an-gels sang a-loud, "Peace on earth," and glo - ry;
4. Stars and an-gels sing a-gain, "Sing the glad-some sto - ry!"

Christ was born in Beth-le-hem, Christ, the King of glo - ry.
Once the Christ, a child like you, Now is King of glo - ry.
To the God who from a - bove Sent this wond'rous sto' - ry.
An - swer to the joy-ous bells, Christ, is King of glo - ry.

CHORUS.

Ring, bells, ring, Christ is King, Christ is King of glo - ry;

Christ is born in Beth-le-hem, Christ, the King of glo - ry.

GRACE J. FRANCES.

HUBERT P. MAIN.

1. How like the fear-ful gi - ant, That Is - rael's host dis-mayed;
2. A - rise! go forth u - nit - ed. Our country's foe to meet;
3. Tho' young, and weak in numbers, We'll stand unmoved and true; -
4. Then on to meet the gi - ant, Nor let our courage fail;

In - temperance now as-sails us, In all his strength arrayed.
Lift up our voice a-gainst him, And pray for his de - feat.
Like him who from the brooklet The shin-ing peb - bles drew.
The Lord our cause de - fending, We sure - ly must pre -vail.

CHORUS.

The arm of our Re - deem-er Will help us strike a blow

That, like the sling in Da- vid's hand, Will lay the ty-rant low.

102 JESUS' LITTLE FRIEND.

Mrs. Clara M. Wilson.   W. H. Doane.

1. I am Je - sus' lit - tle, lit - tle friend, How I love Him,
2. I am hap - py, hap - py all the day, How I love Him,
3. I am sing-ing eve - ry-where I go, How I love Him,
4. In His house are ma-ny mansions fair, How I love Him,

love Him; All I want His gen - tle hand will send, Because He
love Him; Je - sus watch-es, watches o'er my way, And Je - sus
love Him; He will al-ways care for me I know, Because He
love Him; He has told me I may en - ter there, Because He

Refrain.

loves me too.   To His fold how ten - der - ly He guides me,
loves me too.
loves me too.
loves me too.

In His arms He shel-ters now and hides me; I will be His

lit - tle friend for - ev - er, Je - sus loves me too.

PRAISE HIM, PRAISE HIM.

ANON.   Arr. by HUBERT P. MAIN.

1. Praise Him, praise Him, all ye lit - tle chil-dren, He is Love,
2. Love Him, love Him, all ye lit - tle chil-dren, He is Love,

He is Love: Praise Him, praise Him, all ye lit - tle children,
He is Love: Love Him, love Him, all ye lit - tle children,

He is Love, He is love.
He is Love, He is love.

3.
||: Serve Him, serve Him, all ye lit-
tle children,
He is Love, He is Love. :||

4.
||: Crown Him, crown Him, all ye
little children,
He is Love, He is Love. :||

104   SILVER BELLS ARE CHIMING.

FANNY J. CROSBY.   FRED. SCHILLING.

1. Clap your hands re - joic - ing, Grateful tri-bute bring,
2. Tell the bliss-ful ti - dings Heard on Ju-dah's plain,
3. Ev - ery heart is bounding, Ev - ery heart is bright,
4. Bless-ed Lord and Sav-iour, Hear our songs of love,

Hail the Prince of Glo - ry, Hail the new-born King.
Wake the mid - night cho-rus, Shout it forth a - gain.
Mirth and fes - tive pleasure Come with smiles to - night.
Glo - ry in the high-est, Praise to God a - bove.

CHORUS.

Sil - ver bells are chim-ing, Chiming loud and clear,

Mer - ry, mer - ry Christ-mas, Ev - ery-where we hear.

IF WE WANT TO DWELL WITH JESUS. 105

GRACE J. FRANCES.

HUBERT P. MAIN.

1. If we want to dwell with Jesus It must be by grace a-lone;
2. We can nev-er plead our goodness Tho' we serve Him night and day;
3. We are sin - ful, He is ho - ly, We have noth-ing, He has all;
4. If we want to sing with angels In the many man-sions fair,

Not by works nor deeds of kindness That to others we have shown.
We must plead His blessed merits Casting all our own a - way.
Grace has purchased our salvation, Grace redeemed us from the fall.
We must cling by faith to Je - sus, Or we can-not en - ter there.

CHORUS.

Grace a - lone, grace a - lone, We are saved by grace a - lone;

Grace thro' faith in our Redeemer Saves and brings us near His throne.

106 SONG OF THE FLOWERS.

Rev. J. A. COLLIER.   WM. B. BRADBURY.

1. Hark, the lilies whis-per Ten-der-ly and low, "In our grace and
2. Hark, the roses speaking, Tell-ing all abroad Their sweet, wondrous

beau - ty See how fair we grow;" Thus our heavenly Father Cares for
sto - ry, Of the love of God, In the rose of Sharon, Je - sus

all be - low. The lil - ies of the field, The beauti-ful lil - ies
Christ the Lord. The roses how they bloom! The beauti-ful ros - es

of the field, Your Father cares for them, And shall He not care for you?
how they bloom, Your Father, &c.

3 Buttercups and daisies,
  And the violets sweet,
Flowers of field and garden—
  All their voices meet;
And their Maker's praises
  To our souls repeat.
They sing their Maker's praise,
The beautiful flowers, how they
Your Father cares for them, [sing!
And shall He not care for you?

4 Let us, then, be trusted.
  Doubting not, although
Much of toil and trouble
  Be our lot below.
Think upon the lilies,
  See how fair they grow.
The lilies of the field,
The beautiful lilies of the field;
Your Father cares for them,
And shall He not care for you?

BOOK OF GRACE. English.

1. Book of grace, and book of glo-ry, Gift of God to age and youth, Wondrous is thy sa-cred sto-ry, Bright, bright with truth. Wondrous is thy sa-cred sto-ry, Bright, bright with truth.

2. Book of love! in accents ten-der Speaking un-to such as we; May it lead us, Lord, to ren-der All, all to thee, May it lead us, Lord, to ren-der All, all to Thee.

3. Book of hope! the spir-it, sighing, Sweetest comfort finds in thee, As it hears the Saviour cry-ing, "Come, come to Me!" As it hears the Saviour crying, "Come, come to Me!"

108   GOD IS IN HEAVEN.

ANN TAYLOR.   GEO. C. STEBBINS.

1. God is in heaven, can He hear   A   lit- tle pray'r like mine?
2. God is in heaven, would He know If   I should tell a   lie?
3. God is in heaven, may I   go   To ask Him for His care?

Yes, that He can; I   will not fear; He'll lis-ten un-to   mine.
Yes, tho' I said it ver - y   low, He'd hear it in   the sky.
. Not yet, but love Him here be-low, And He will see it there.

God is   in heaven, can He see   When I am do - ing wrong?
God is   in heaven, does He care, And   is He good to   me?
God is   in heaven, may I pray To   go there when I die?

Yes, that He can; He looks at me   All day and all night long.
Yes; all I have to   eat and wear, 'Tis God that gives it me.
Yes; trust and serve Him, and one day He'll call me to the sky.

ANON.   PHILIP PHILLIPS, by per.

1. I oft - en think of heathen lands,—Far, far a - way! Where
2. O how I pit - y children there,—Far, far a - way! Al -
3. But I will pray that God may send—Far, far a - way, Glad

high the pa - gan tem-ple stands.—Far, far a - way; And
though the clime be pass-ing fair,— Far, far a - way; I
ti - dings of my Saviour Friend—Far, far a - way; And

there each hapless child is led To bow to i - dol gods his
would not leave my native home, In fields of rich-est fruit to
ev - ery lit - tle I can spare Shall help to send the Bi - ble

head, While many mutt'ring charms are said, Far, far a - way!
roam, If there no gospel light should come,—Far, far a - way!
there, And men of God the truth to bear Far, far a - way!

PRAISE GOD FOR THE BIBLE.

Rev. W. F. CRAFTS.   Sir H. R. BISHOP.

1. Praise God for the Bi-ble Which comes like a friend, To counsel and
2. Praise God for the Bi - ble, The mir-ror of sin; That shows us our
3. Praise God for the Bi - ble, It burns like a fire, As dross from the

com - fort, To guide and defend; Praise God for the Bi - ble, Far
wrongness Without and within; Praise God for the Bi - ble, The
sil - ver, Each e - vil de-sire; Praise God for the Bi - ble, His

D. S.—*Praise God for the Bi - ble That*

better than gold, The words of sure promise, Its pages un - fold.
water of truth, Which gladdens and cleanses The way of our youth.
let - ter of love, To fathers and children, In-vi - ting a-bove.
gladdens our days.

FINE.

CHORUS.   D. S. *for Chorus.*

Praise, praise, forev-er praise,

4 Praise God for the Bible,
  That kills like a sword,
Our sins and wrong doings,
  And fights for the Lord;
Praise God for the Bible,
  A lamp in our path,
To guide through life's journey
  And shadow of death.

J. C. F.

WM. F. SHERWIN.

1. Car - ol, sweet - ly ca - rol, Hap - py songs to - day;
2. An - gels o'er His cra - dle Watch'd with ten-der care;
3. Mer - ry, mer - ry Christmas, Joy - ful let us sing;

FINE.

Cher - ub voic - es min - gle In our fes - tive lay.
Ra - diant beams of glo - ry Shone in beau-ty there.
Glo - ry in the high-est, Chist the Lord is King!

Christ the lov - ing Sav - iour, Gen - tle, pure and mild;
Wise men came to wor - ship, Guid-ed by a star,
Glo - ry in the high-est To His name be given;

ritard. D.C.

Came from heav'n to save us, Came a lit - tle child.
Bring-ing gold - en treasures From a land a - far.
Glo - ry in the high-est! Praise Him earth and heaven!

112 FALLING, FALLING, EVER FALLING.

GRACE J. FRANCES.   HUBERT P. MAIN.

1. Fall-ing, fall - ing, ev - er   fall - ing From our Father's
2. Fall-ing, fall - ing, ev - er   fall - ing With each moment's
3. Fall-ing, fall - ing, ev - er   fall - ing, Ten-der words of

throne a - bove, Like the gen - tle dew   of Sum-mer, Precious
wan-ing light, Some new pleasure un - ex - pect-ed Fills the
hap - py cheer, From the bless-ed lips of Je - sus, To   re -

CHORUS.

gifts of   ten - der love. Fall-ing, fall-ing, ev - er fall-ing;
soul with strange de-light.
fresh His child-ren here.

In our heart some precious blessing, From our Fa - ther's throne a - bove, Falls in mer - cy, falls in love.

THE LORD'S PRAYER.

Our Father, who art in heaven, | hallowed| be Thy|name.
Give us this | day our. |dai - ly | bread.
And lead us not into temptation, but de-|liv - er | us from| evil:

Thy kingdom come. Thy will be done in |earth as it |is in |heav'n.
And forgive us our debts, as |we for-|give our |debtors.
For Thine is the kingdom, and the power,
    and the |glory, for-|ever. A|men.

GLORIA PATRI.

Glory be to the Father, and |to the | Son, || and | to the | Holy|Ghost;
As it was in the beginning,
    is now, and |ever|shall be,||world |without|end.A|men.

114   I LOVE THEM THAT LOVE ME.

Proverbs 8: 17.   HUBERT P. MAIN.

I love them, I love them, I love them that love Me, I love

them that love Me; and those that seek Me ear - ly, and those that

seek Me ear - ly, and those that seek Me ear-ly, shall find Me.

Tune—"Balerma." C. M.

1 Remember Thy Creator now,
  In these Thy youthful days;
He will accept Thy earliest vow,
  And listen to Thy praise.

2 Remember Thy Creator now,
  And seek Him while He's near,
For evil days will come, when Thou
  Shalt find no comfort here.

3 Remember Thy Creator now;
  His willing servant be;
Then, when Thy head in death shall
  He will remember Thee. [bow,

4 Almighty God! our hearts incline
  Thy heavenly voice to hear;
Let all our future days be Thine,
  Devoted to Thy fear.

Chanted alternately by the boys and girls, or by half of the school.

R. FARRANT, 1570.

Christ our Passover is................... | sacri-ficed | for us:
Not with the old leaven, neither with
          the leaven of | malice and|wickedness;
Christ being raised from the dead,.. .... | dieth no | more;
For in that He died, He died unto........ | sin........ | once;
Likewise reckon ye also yourselves to be
          dead in - | deed unto | sin,
Christ is risen........................ | from the | dead.
For since by........................| man came | death,
For as in.............................| Adam all | die,

therefore...................... | let us | keep the | feast.
but with the unleavened bread of sin-| cer - i - | ty and | truth.
death hath no more do- - - | min - ion | o - ver | Him.
but in that He liveth, He........ | liv - eth | un - to | God.
but alive unto God through....... | Je - sus |Christ our | Lord.
and become the first............ | fruits of |them that | slept.
by man came also the resur- - - |rec - tion | of the |dead.
even so in Christ shall all be...... |made a- | live. A- | men.

116   OPENING.—Chant.

Rev. J. B. ATCHINSON.   W. H. DOANE.

1. Saviour, at Thy throne we bow;   Oh, |come and|meet us | now;
2. While we learn from out Thy Word, Oh, |grant Thy|Spir-it,|Lord;

Let Thy blessing, Lord, we pray, Rest up-|on our|class to-|day.
Help us each and every one: This we |ask thro'|Christ Thy|Son. Amen.

CLOSING.—Chant.

Rev. J. B. ATCHINSON.   W. H. DOANE.

1. Dear Saviour, ere we part, We |lift our |hearts to|Thee
2. Go with us to our homes,   Watch |o'er and|keep us |there,

In gratitude and praise,   For |blessings|full and|free.
And make us one and all, The |children|of Thy|care. A-men.

SONGS FOR SCHOOL AND HOME.

THE BONNIE BIT OF BLUE,

ANON.

"AULD LANG SYNE."

1. Of all the tints the light looks on, Howev-er bright their hue,
2. Come, wear the blue—you cannot know The good that you may do,
3. Then wear the blue above the heart That's brave, and warm and true,

There's none that speaks of better things Than does the bit of blue.
By join-ing in a no - ble cause, The Ar-my of the blue.
And nev - er be a-shamed to show The bonnie bit of blue.
D. S.—*It tells of hope, it tells of joy, The bon - nie bit of blue.*

REFRAIN.

D.S.

The bon - nie bit of blue, my friends, The bonnie bit of blue,

THE MORNING SUN IS SHINING.

ANON.

German.

1. The morn-ing sun is shin - ing bright, How fair and
2. The Lord has spared us through the night, That we might

gold - en is the light; 'Twas God who sent him on his
see the morn-ing light; Oh, may we try at work and

way To give us warmth and light to - day.
play To please Him this and ev - ery day.

LITTLE BIRD YOU ARE WELCOME. .

T. E. HEERWART.

ANON.

1. Lit - tle bird you are wel - come, What news do you
2. A...... kiss and a let - ter I bring you to
3. Take... our moth - er one word And that is our

MOTION SONG—See page 156.

bring From our mother and home? Now tell us and sing.
day, If you've something better I'll take it a - way.
love; Fly a - way, gen-tle bird. Fly a-way gen-tle dove.

BIRDIES IN THE WOOD.

ANON.   A. WEBER.

1. Bird-ies in the wood, Mer - ri - ly do sing;
2. Bird-ies in the wood, Safe-ly build their nest;
3. Bird-ies in the wood Soon will si - lence keep;

For their hap - py lives Joy and gladness bring.
Hid - den in the trees, We will let them rest.
Soft - ly, gent - ly sing, For they all will sleep.

|1st. | 2d. |

Tra la la, Tra la la, Tra la la; La la la, Tra la. Tra la,

MOTION SONG—see page 156.

120   SEE THE CHICKENS ROUND THE GATE.

Mrs. D. A. Thrupp.   Fr. Seidel.

1. See the chickens round the gate, For their morning portion wait;
2. Ea - ger, bus - y hen and chick, Ev - ery lit - tle mor-sel pick;
3. As she calls, they flock around, Bustling all a-long the ground;

Fill   the basket from the store, O - pen wide the cot-tage door;
See   the hen with callow brood, To her young how kind and good,
When their dai - ly la-bors cease, And at night they rest in peace;

Throw out crumbs and scatter seed, Let the hungry chickens feed;
With what care their steps she leads, Them, and not herself, she feeds;
All   the lit - tle ti - ny things, Nes-tle close beneath her wings;

Call them now, how fast they run, Gladly, quick-ly, ev - ery one.
Pick-ing here, and pick-ing there, Where the nic-est mor-sels are.
Then she keeps them safe and warm, Free from fear and free from harm.

Motion Song—See page 156.

THE SPRING IS COME.

(ROUND IN THREE PARTS.)

The spring is come, I hear the birds That sing from bush to bush;

Hark!   hark!   I   hear them sing:

The lin - net and the lit - tle wren, The blackbird and the thrush.

SWEETLY NOW THE BELLS.

(ROUND IN THREE PARTS.)

Sweet - ly   now   the   bells   are   ring - ing.   Call   to

church   for   prayer and   sing - ing.   Ding, dong, ding, dong.

HE WHO WOULD LEAD.

(ROUND IN TWO PARTS.)

He who would lead a hap - py life,   He who would lead a

hap - py life, Must   keep   him - self   from   an - gry

strife, from an - gry   strife, from an - gry strife.

MY DOG DASH.

ANON.   THEODORE E. PERKINS, by per.

1. My dog Dash is full of fun,   Bow, wow, wow, wow, wow;
2. Now he's romping far a - way,   Bow, wow, wow, wow, wow;

See him jump, and roll, and run, Bow, wow, wow, wow, wow;
Now he's roll-ing in the hay, Bow, wow, wow, wow, wow;

Lis - ten to his joy-ous bark, Bow, wow, wow, wow, wow;
Bet - ter dog you ne'er did see, Bow, wow, wow, wow, wow;

As he scampers thro' the park, Bow, wow, wow, wow, wow.
I love Dash and Dash loves me, Bow, wow, wow, wow, wow.

I KNOW.   123

ISABELLA F. BELLOWS.
Rev. R. LOWRY.

1. Where do all the dai - ses go? I know, I know!
2. Where do all the bird - ies go? I know, I know!
3. Where do all the ba - bies go? I know, I know!

Un-der-neath the snow they creep, Nod their lit-tle heads and sleep;
Far a - way from winter snow, To the fair, warm South they go;
In the glancing fire-light warm, Shelter'd safe from ev-ery harm,

In the spring-time out they peep—That is where they go.
There they stay till dai - sies blow—That is where they go.
Soft they lie on mother's arm— That is where they go.

Tune—"Webb." 7. 6.

1 We wont give up the Bible,
  God's holy book divine,
The Book of inspiration,
  Where truth and wisdom shine;
No hand shall wrest it from us,
  No tyrant power we fear,
We wont give up the Bible,
  Our Fathers loved so dear.

2 We wont give up the Bible,
  That tells a Saviour's love,
The precious Lamp that guides us,
  To purer joys above;
We wont give up the Bible,
  But read it day by day,
God help us by its counsel,
  To find the narrow way.

124 RAIN DROPS.

Arr. from Mrs. HAYWOOD.　　　　　　　Music and v. 3 by H. R. PALMER.

1. Pet is at the window pane, Watching lit - tle drops of rain;
2. Thoughtfully she lifts her eyes Up-ward to the darkened skies;
3. "Do the angels," darling said, "Cry because they're put to bed?

On the glass they pit-ter pat-ter; Dar-ling wonders what's the
Earnest - ly and long she gaz-es; Ver - y sad her lit - tle
Are they sometimes very naughty, Just like—just like—lit - tle

mat-ter; As she turns and questions "Why, mamma, do the
face is; As she turns and questions "Why, mamma, do the
Lottie?" Thus the dar - ling questions "Why, mamma, do the

Ad lib.　　　　　　　　　　　　*A little faster.*

angels cry?" "Mamma, mamma, Do the angels cry?"
angels cry?" "Mamma, mamma, Do the angels cry?"
angels cry?" "Mamma, mamma, Do the angels cry?"

MOTION SONG—See page 157. Copyright, 1883, by H. R. Palmer.

GO TO SLEEP, MY DARLING BABY. 125

Mrs. CHARLOTTE B. MERRITT.   HUBERT P. MAIN.

Slowly.

1. Go to sleep, my darling ba - by, Cud-dle down and go to rest;
2. All the birds and flowers sleeping, Watched by stars and bath'd in dew;

Nestle here where heart-throbs tell you, You are safe on mamma's breast.
Then, my ba - by, no more peeping With those precious eyes of blue.

REFRAIN.

Bye - o - ba - by, bye - o - ba - by, You are safe on mamma's breast.

3 Go to sleep, my darling baby,
  Shut your pretty little eyes;
Till the morning finds my darling
  Waiting for the sun to rise.

4 Birds and flowers will call you early,
  Calling in the first pink light;
Wake up, baby, hear the birdies
  Singing songs about the night.

5 Hear them tell how all the sunlight
  Went far down beyond the west;
But a piece of moon was shining,
  And a star o'er every nest.

6 So the birdies slept, my darling,
  Trusting in the silver bow,
For the promise of the sunshine,
  And the birds were right, you know.

126 WHEN THE MORNING LIGHT.

R. L.

Rev. R. Lowry, by per.

1. When the morning light drives a - way the night, With the
2. In the class I meet with the friends I greet, At the
3. May the dews of grace fill the hallowed place, And the

sun so bright and full, And the day of rest lightens
time of ope-ning pray'r; And our hearts we raise in a
sun-shine nev - er fail, While each blooming rose which in

ev - ery breast, I'll a - way to Sab-bath school; For 'tis
hymn of praise, For 'tis al - ways pleasant there; In the
memory grows, Shall a sweet per-fume ex - hale; When we

there we all a-gree, All with happy hearts and free, And I
Book of ho - ly truth, Full of coun - sel and reproof, We be-
min - gle here no more, But have met on Jordan's shore, We will

GIRLS.

love to ear - ly be At the Sab-bath school; I'll a -
hold the guide of youth, At the Sab-bath school; I'll, &c.
talk of moments o'er At the Sab-bath school; I'll, &c.

BOYS. GIRLS. BOYS. ALL.

way! a - way! I'll a-way! a - way! I'll a-way to Sabbath school.

THE SUN IS IN THE WEST.

J. BURTON. From MENDELSSOHN.

1. The sun is in the west; The close of day I see;
2. I'll thank Him for His love, That kept me thro' the day;
3. Then I can fall a - sleep, And close my slumbering eyes,

I go to take my rest; The Lord has cared for me.
He'll lis - ten from a - bove, And hear me when I pray.
For lov - ing watch will keep, My Fa-ther up on high.

THE TREES.

Miss WEBB.   German.

1.
{ See the trees all in a row, Gent-ly swaying to and fro; }
{ Hark! the wind is ris-ing now, And the trees be-fore it bow; }

How their creaking branches sound, While the leaves are scattered round;

Now the pass-ing storm is o'er, Qui - et - ly they stand once more.

MOTION SONG—See page 157.

SEE, MY LITTLE BIRDIE'S NEST.

A. KOEHLER.   German.
                                                   FINE.

1. See, my lit - tle birdie's nest, And an egg in it does rest;
D. C. Egg in nest so snug doth lie, Bird-ie will come by and by.
2. Save the nest and spare the egg, Do not touch it, this I beg;
D. C. It will sing to you a song, This will please you all day long.

MOTION SONG—See page 157.

D.C.

But the lit-tle bird has flown, To the greenwood he has gone;
When the bird comes home again, Let it find its nest, and then

THE WINDMILL.

FR. SEIDEL.

FR. SEIDEL.

The wind must blow to turn the mill, Or else it will stand still, stand still;

The corn makes meal, the meal makes bread, That all the people may be

fed; The wind must blow to turn the mill, Or else it will stand still.

Motion Song—See page 157.

130 THE LAMBKIN.

ERNEST ANSCHUTZ.   A. WEBER.

1. In the grass-y pla - ces, Where the flow'rs are seen,
2. On the sun - ny pas - ture Mer - ri - ly she springs,
3. Where the birds are singing, To the brook she goes,
4. Soft-ly there she rests her By the run - ing stream;
5. Like the lambkin love-ly, From all e - vil free;

There the lamb-kin gra - zes, On the ten - der green.
Feels, like us, the pleasure Sun-shine ev - er brings.
And when she's done drinking, Then she seeks re - pose.
We will not mo - lest her, Sweet-ly let her dream.
Kind and good and low - ly, I would ev - er be.

BLINDFOLDED.

Miss WEBB.   ANON.

1. There's a flow'r with-in my hand; Can you tell what it may be?
2. If you say the proper name—Guessing by the scent a-lone—

MOTION SONG—See page 157.

But I hope you understand, You may smell but must not see.
You a sweet reward may claim, For the flow'r shall be your own.

SEE THE RAIN IS FALLING.

ANON. ANON.

1. See the rain is fall - ing On the mountain's side!
2. See the cool - ing show - er Comes at God's com-mand,

See the clouds dis - pers - ing Blessings far and wide.
Brightens ev - ery flow - er, Cheers the parch-ed land.

3 When the rain is over,
Then the painted bow
O'er the cloudy hill-top
Will its colors show.

4 God is ever faithful,
God is ever true;
Let us all be thankful
For the rain and dew.

132   IF EARLY TO BED.

ANON.

1. If ear - ly to bed, and ear - ly to rise, You'll be, as they
2. 'Tis good for your health, 'tis good for your purse, No doctor you'll

tell me, both healthy and wise; If health you would keep, this
need, and but sel-dom a nurse; Then ear - ly to bed, and

counsel you'll take, Be ear-ly a - sleep and be ear-ly a-wake.
ear - ly to rise, If you would be healthy and wealthy and wise.

BRIGHTLY GLOWS THE DAY.

J. CURWEN.

1. Bright-ly glows the day, Night has fled a - way.
2. Sweet is morn to me, Thanks, O God, to Thee!
3. Hear me while I raise, This my song of praise;

Ev - ery joy - ful sound Ech - oes all a - round.
Thou a guard hast kept, O'er me while I slept.
May my heart each day, To Thee ev - er pray.

LOOK AT THE CLOCKS.

WUCKE. ARTES.

1. Look at the clocks dear children, How much they have to do;
2. The clock on yon high tow - er, How stead-y does it go;

In autumn and in win - ter, In spring and summer too.
In sunshine and in show-er, It always sounds just so.

Tic, tac, tic, tac, tic, tac.

3 At home, with equal measure,
The clock ticks in the hall;
To listen, gives us pleasure,
For it will always call.
4 But hark! my little ticker
It is in constant flight;
Although it sounds much quicker,
It shows the time aright.

MOTION SONG—See page 157.

134   LITTLE BO-PEEP.

Anon.

Arr. from J. W. Elliott.

1. Lit-tle Bo-Peep has lost her sheep, And can't tell where to find them
2. Lit-tle Bo-Peep fell fast asleep, And dreamt she heard them bleating,
3. Then up she took her little crook, Determined sure to find them;

Cres.   f

Leave them alone, and they'll come home, Wagging their tails behind them.
When she a - woke 'twas all a joke, Ah! cru-el vision so fleeting.
What was her joy to behold them nigh, Wagging their tails behind them.

GOD IS ALWAYS NEAR ME.

J. Burton.

H. Weichert.

1. God is al-ways near me, Hear-ing what I say;
2. God is al-ways near me, In the dark - est night;
3. God is al-ways near me, Though so young and small;

GOD IS ALWAYS NEAR ME.—Concluded. 135

Know-ing all my tho'ts and deeds, All my work and play.
He can see me just the same, As by mid-day light.
Not a look, or word, or thought, But God knows it all.

GOD SPEED THE RIGHT.

W. E. HICKSON.   German.

1. Now to heaven our prayer ascending, God speed the right; In a no - ble
2. Be that prayer a-gain re-peat-ed, God speed the right; Ne'er de-spairing,
3. Pa-tient, firm, and per - se-ver-ing; God speed the right; Ne'er th'event nor

cause contending, God speed the right.   Be our zeal in heaven record-ed,
though de-feat-ed, God speed the right.   Like the good and great in sto-ry,
dan - ger fear-ing, God speed the right.   Pains, nor toils, nor tri-als heed-ing,

With suc-cess on earth re-ward-ed, God speed the right, God speed the right.
If we fail, we fail with glo - ry, God speed the right, God speed the right.
In the strength of heaven succeeding—God speed the right, God speed the right.

A PRIMARY SERVICE.

BY MRS. M. G. KENNEDY.

Teacher. The Lord is in His holy temple.
Scholars. Let all the earth keep silence before Him

OPENING CHANT—p. 116.

PRAYER SERVICE

T. What is prayer?
S. Prayer is asking God for what we wish, from the heart, and thanking Him for what He has done for us.
T. To whom should we pray?
S. To our Father in heaven, who is the giver of all good and perfect gifts.

PRAYER SONG. (Softly.) "I will pray." p. 94.

PRAYER.—Closing with Lord's Prayer in concert.

GIFT SERVICE.

T. What sort of a giver does God love?
S. The Lord loveth a cheerful giver.
T. What has the Lord given us?
S. God so loved the world that He gave His only begotten Son etc.

CONCERT RECITATION.—Sunday Collection.

> Small are the gifts that we can bring.
> But thou hast taught us, Lord,
> If given for the Saviour's sake,
> They lose not their reward.

SINGING "LITTLE GIVERS." Songs for Little Folks. p. 81.

SCRIPTURE SERVICE—Recitation, on alternate Sabbaths, of Commandments Beatitudes, or 23d Psalm.

MOVEMENT SONG.—"The child's gift to God" p. 63.

RECITATION OF GOLDEN TEXTS, for Quarter or Year.

LESSON SERVICE.

T. From what book are all our lessons taken?
S. From God's blessed book, the Bible

T. If it is God's Word, how should we listen?

S. (Touching parts named.) With our *eyes,* that we may see; with our *ears,* that we may hear; with our *hearts,* that we may do the things which we are taught.

BIBLE HYMN. "God's blessed Book." p. 31.

LESSON REVIEW. Last Lesson.

HYMN. "Come, learn of the Meek and Lowly." p. 44.

T. "Come ye children, hearken unto me, and I will teach you the fear of the Lord.

S. I will hear what the Lord will speak.

LESSON TAUGHT. (Lesson for the Day.)

LESSON HYMN. Suitable to subject.

LESSON FINISHED—or reviewed by Sup't.

LESSON PRAYER. (Softly.) "Heavenly Father, grant thy blessing."—p. 151.

Distribution of papers, etc.

PARTING WORDS.

T. "The Lord bless thee and keep thee."

S. "The Lord watch between me and thee when we are absent one from another.

CHILDREN'S PRAISE SERVICE.

BY MRS. M. G. KENNEDY.

Teacher. I was glad when they said unto me, "Let us go into the house of the Lord."

Children. "This is the day which the Lord hath made; we will rejoice and be glad in it."

T. Serve the Lord with gladness.

C. Come before His presence with singing.

HYMN.—"Sing always"—p. 17.

T. Enter into His gates with thanksgiving;

C. And into His courts with praise.

T. Be thankful unto Him, and bless His name

C. O, Lord, open Thou my lips, and my mouth shall show forth Thy praise

PRAISE PRAYER.—(Sing softly.) "Jesus, high in glory,"—p. 46.

T. Let the people praise Thee, O, God;

C. Let all the people praise Thee.

T. Both young men and maidens ;
C. Old men and children.
All. Let them praise the name of the Lord, for His name alone is excellent ;
His glory is above the earth and heaven.
CHILDREN'S GLORIA. "Glory to the Father give." p. 20.
Concert Recitations, *with motions*, of Ps. 148 : 1-10.
SINGING—"Hark ! the Lark is singing." p. 16
T. O, magnify the Lord with me.
C. And let us exalt His name together.
HYMN. "Day by day." p. 75.
T. Out of the mouths of babes and sucklings thou hast perfected praise.
C. Hosanna to the son of David !
HYMN. "Children's thanks." p. 67.
T. Let us give praises for God's best gift. "For God so loved the world,
etc.
C. Thanks be unto God for His unspeakable gift. John 3 : 16.
HYMN. "Blessed, blessed Jesus." p. 9.
[This service may be interspersed with brief prayers and remarks.]

THE CHILDREN'S CHAUTAUQUA DRILL.

v. 1. Right hand raised.—"Lift your hands in the sanctuary, and bless the
Lord."
v. 2. Clap hands once —"O. clap your hands, all ye people."
v. 3. Fold arms.—"Thy word have I hid in mine heart."
v. 4. Stand up.—"Stand up and bless the Lord your God."
v. 5. Join tips of fingers over head.—"His banner over me was love."
v. 6. Put hands by the sides.—"Happy is the man that findeth wisdom."
v. 7. Right hand stretched out.—"Length of days is in her right hand."
v. 8. Left hand stretched out.—"And in her left hand riches and honor."
v. 9. Clap hands three times.—"Her ways are ways of pleasantness, and all
her paths are peace."
v. 10. Sit down.—"Him that overcometh will I grant to sit with me in my
throne."

EASTER PRAISES.

SINGING—"Lift up, O little children." p. 64, v. 1.

Teacher.—Sons of men and angels say,
    Raise your joys and triumphs high.

Hal - le - lu - jah! Hal - le - lu - jah!

Teacher.—

Love's redeeming work is done,
Fought the fight, the victory won ;
Jesus' agony is o'er,
Darkness veils the earth no more.

Vain the stone, the watch, the seal,
Christ has burst the gates of hell !
Death in vain forbids His rise,
Christ hath opened paradise

Hal - le - lu - jah! Hal - le - lu - jah! Hal - le - lu - jah!

Recitation of Scripture texts by individual children.

"He is risen."—*Matt.* 14: 2.
"The Lord is risen indeed."—*Luke* 24: 34.
"I know that my Redeemer liveth."—*Job* 19: 25.
"The Lord is King forever and ever."—*Ps.* 10: 16.
"O Death, where is thy sting? O Grave, where is thy victory."—1 *Cor.* 15: 55.
"Death is swallowed up in victory."—1 *Cor.* 15: 54.
"Alleluia! Alleluia! Alleluia!"—*Rev.* 19: 1, 3, 4.
"Thou hast ascended on high, and hast led captivity captive."—*Ps.* 68: 18.
"Christ was raised again from justification."—*Rom.* 4: 25.
"I am the Resurrection and the Life."—*John* 11: 25.
"As in Adam all die, even so in Christ shall all be made alive."—1 *Cor.* 15: 22.
"Now is Christ risen from the dead, and become the first fruits of them that slept."—1 *Cor.* 15: 20.
"Alleluia! for the Lord God omnipotent reigneth."—*Rev.* 19: 6.

SINGING—"Lilies! Lilies! Easter calls." p. 87, v. 2.

Recitation by five groups of little girls dressed in white, each holding the lily she represents.

All together.

" We are lilies every one,
Nodding brightly to the sun."

Meadow Lilies. (four or five little girls in a group.)

"We are lilies looking down,
Modest in our glistening gown."

Water Lilies.

"We are lilies of the lake.
Never more than half awake."

Lillies of the Valley. (by a group of tiny girls.)

"Little lilies of the vale,
God hath made us very frail;"

"Yet we give
Love to all the flowers that grow,
And the flowers love us so:
We are happier than you know,
Just to live."

Day Lilies.

"Surely we are born in state,
But our honors will not wait,
And our life, early and late,
Is a day."

Calla Lilies.

"Lilies, lilies, list you all,
We are Easter lilies tall."

SINGING—"Lift up, O tender Lilies."   p. 64, v. 2.

Recitation by a little child.

"Now tell the little children
How Christ our Saviour, too,
The Flower of all eternity,
Once death and darkness knew."

"How, like these blossoms, silent
Within the tomb He lay.
Then rose in light and glory,
To live in heaven for aye."

Recitation by the Lilies.

"Now upon the first day of the week." etc.—*Luke* 24: 1, 6.

SINGING—"Waken, sleeping butterflies."   p. 87, v. 3.

Recitation by the Class.

Soar we now where Christ hath led,
Following our exalted Head:
Made like Him, like Him we rise;
Ours the cross, the grave, the skies.

SINGING—"Ring, all ye bells."   p. 64, v. 3.

Sung by the whole Class, each child with some sort of a lily in hand with which to imitate the ringing of a bell.

CHILDREN'S DAY.

JESUS AND THE CHILDREN.

SINGING . "Our Hearts are Young and Joyous." p. 26.

TEACHER: Nearly two thousand years ago, Jesus Christ began life in this world as a baby. I say in this world, because the Bible tells us that He was alive before he came into this world. You and I were nothing at all until we were born. But Jesus Christ was the Son of God "before He became the Son of Man." There are many places in the Bible where He is said to have lived in great glory before man was made, or angels either.

Why did Jesus Christ become a child?

Recitation by a little child:

" The Son of God knows what it is to be a child, to think as a child, to speak as a child, to understand as a child, to feel as a child. As a child, he lay upon his mother's lap, and looked up smilingly into his mother's face. As a child, he had his childish games, and shed his childish tears. As a child, he had to put up with little troubles, and found his lessons sometimes hard, and met with many things that he could not understand. And he remembers all this, and can enter into the feelings of little children. He became a child that he might do so."

SINGING: " All our little heartaches." p. 21.

SINGING: SOLO AND CHORUS: " Jesus Once was a little Child." p. 24.

Recitation by a little child:

Jesus says, " It is not the will of your Father in Heaven that one of these little ones should perish;" and also that " The Son of Man is come to seek and to save that which was lost. And then he goes on to say that if a man has a hundred sheep, and one of them goes astray, he leaves them all to seek that one, and if he finds it, he has more joy in it than all of the rest. And so the Good Shepherd rejoices when he finds those who have wandered from his fold, whether sheep or lambs. WE NEED SAVING IN THIS WAY. The youngest who turn right from wrong need it. ' We all like sheep have gone astray,' and must return to the ' Shepherd of our souls.' That is *Salvation*, the being found by Jesus, and brought back to the fold. It means being made good and happy in God's love."

SINGING: SOLO AND CHORUS: " Little Ones Like Me." p. 52.

Recitation: " Suffer little children, and forbid them not to come unto me; for of such is the kingdom of heaven."

SINGING: "O When We Remember," p. 10.

Recitation :

When Jesus said ' Feed my lambs,' he meant *little ones.* He might have called all of his disciples lambs, but he did not do so, for just afterward he said ' Feed my sheep.'

The Bible has milk for babies, that is, easy thoughts for little children to understand. These are what God would have our parents and teachers feed ' our souls with.

SINGING, SOLO: " Very little do we know." p. 28.

Recitation : The Twenty-third Psalm, by the class in concert.

Recitation by a child :

" A good shepherd does not treat all of his sheep alike. Some are old, some are young; some are strong, some are weak; some are well, some are sick. Some have the use of all their limbs, some have suffered from accidents, and are torn or lame. God's complaint against the shepherds of Israel was : The diseased have ye not strengthened, neither have ye healed that which was sick, neither have ye bound up that which was broken, neither have ye brought, again that which was driven away, neither have ye sought that which was lost.' Jesus Christ does all these things, and all other things needed by his flock. He knows them all, knows their hearts, and histories and circumstances. In him all fullness dwells, all wisdom, power, and grace; and out of his fullness they all receive."

SINGING: " Our Shepherd. " p. 15.

A MISSIONARY SERVICE.

SCRIPTURE RECITATION with motions by the whole class.

Wherefore should the heathen say, Where *is* now their God?

But our God *is* in the heavens *(Children point upwards)*: he hath done whatsoever he hath pleased.

Their idols *are* silver and gold, the work of men's hand *(Hands extended).*

They have mouths *(Point to mouths)*, but they speak not : eyes have they, but they see not *(Hands on eyes).*

They have ears, but they hear not *(Touch ears)*: noses have they, but they smell not *(Touch noses).*

They have hands, but they handle not *(Hands extended)*: feet have they, but they walk not *(Point to feet)*: neither speak they through their throat.

They that make them are like unto them; *so is* every one that trusteth in them

SINGING: "The First Commandment." p. 34.

RECITATION by two little boys:

1ST CHILD.

We plead for the little children,
 Who have opened their baby eyes
In the far-off lands of darkness
 Where the shadow of death yet lies.

But not to be nurtured for heaven,
 Not to be taught in the way,
Not to be watched o'er and guided,
 Lest their tiny feet should stray.

Ah, no! It is idol worship
 Their stammering lips are taught;
To cruel, false gods only
 Are their gifts and offerings brought.

And what can *we* children offer,
 Who dwell in this Christian land?
Is there no work for the Master
 In reach of each little hand?

2ND CHILD.

Oh! surely a hundred tapers
 Which even small fingers can clasp
May lighten as much of the darkness
 As a lamp in a stronger grasp.

And then, as the line grows longer,
 So many tapers, though small,
May kindle a brighter shining
 Than a lamp would, after all.

Small hands may gather rich treasures,
 And even infant lips can pray;
Employ, then, the little fingers
 Let the children learn the way.

So the lights shall be quicker kindled,
 And darkness the sooner shall flee:
Many "little ones" learn of the Saviour
 Both here and "far over the sea."

SINGING: "There's a Friend" p. 76. 70057

DIALOGUE for a very little boy and girl:

BOY.
Once there was a little boy; and what do you think he had?

GIRL.
A bright new ten-cent scrip; and I tell you he was glad.

BOY.
Once there was a little scrip; and where did it find itself?

GIRL.
Dropped in the mission-fund in the bank on the parlor shelf.

BOY.
Once there was a mission-fund; and where do you think it went?

GIRL.
To buy some nice new books to be to the heathen sent.

BOY.
Once there was a little book that was bought with the bright new scrip;

GIRL.
That went to a mission-school in a box in the mission ship.

BOY.
Once there was a heathen child; and what do you think, said he?

GIRL.
"I thank the boy who gave his scrip to buy a book for me."

BOY.
Once there was a little boy; I wish it had been myself.

GIRL.
Then put your scrip in the mission-fund in the bank on the parlor shelf.

SINGING, SOLO AND CHORUS: "The Little Missionary." v. 38.

Speech by a little boy:

I think missionaries must have a pretty hard time, for they have to leave their dear friends to go to live among people who would like to eat them up, but not because they love them so much. They must think that a white man is pretty good eating. A missionary would not be quite to my taste!

All missionaries, however, are not white; some are red, or copper colored. This kind has neither eyes nor ears, feet nor hands; and yet it is very remarkable how much they can do for the heathen.

I have invited a great many of these to be present this evening as dumb orators. One hundred or more have reported, and they are now hiding under my handkerchief. They will soon sail for India or some other mission station. They would like to be joined by many more, because they are very small, and each one could do only a little. I will now introduce them to you. (Lifts up the handkerchief which has been covering some coins).

This is Mr. One Cent; here is another of the same name, and here is another, and another.

Here is one called "Two Cents." He can do just twice as much as One Cent.

Everybody here is rich enough to send several of the missionaries, and when the contribution box is passed, I confidently expect to see the company one hundred swelled to a regiment.

Recitation by a girl:

HOW MUCH DO I COST YOU?

A little daughter, ten years old, lay on her death bed. It was hard to part with the pet of the family; the golden hair, the loving blue eyes, the bird-like voice, the truthful, affectionate child. How could she be given up? Between this child and her father there had always existed, not a relationship merely, but the love of congenial natures. He fell on his knees beside his darling's bedside, and wept bitter tears. He strove to say, but could not: "Thy will be done." It was a conflict between grace and nature, such as he had never before experienced. His sobs disturbed the child, who had been lying apparently unconscious. She opened her eyes and looked distressed.

"Papa, dear papa," she said at length.

"What, my darling?" asked her father, striving for composure.

"Papa," she said, in faint, broken tones, "how much do I cost you every year?"

"Hush, dear, be quiet;" he replied, in great agitation, for he feared delirium was coming on.

"But please, papa, how much do I cost you?"

To soothe her he replied, though with a shaking voice: "Well. dearest, perhaps two hundred dollars. What then, darling?"

"Because, papa, 1 thought maybe you would lay it out this year in something for poor children to remember me by."

A beam of heavenly joy glanced in the father's heart—the joy of one noble spirit mingled with its like. Self was forgotten—the sorrow of parting, the lonely future. Naught remained but the mission of love, and a thrill of gratitude that he and his beloved were co-workers.

COLLECTION and Organ Offertory.

CHANT: " Gloria Patri." p. 113.

A TEMPERANCE CONCERT.

SINGING: " Our Temperance Army." p. 91.

(Let this be sung as the children march to the platform, headed by one bearing a banner with the inscription: " TREMBLE, TYRANTS, WE SHALL GROW UP." Let the motto be made of gold letters and fastened to our national flag).

SPEECH by the ensign :

I will explain to you the meaning of our flag, In France, when wicked tyrants were kings. some of the boys formed a Band of Hope. and marched through the streets with these words on their flags : " Tremble, tyrants, we shall grow up." Perhaps the king laughed when he saw them, and thought it boys' play. But it was no idle boast. They did make the king tremble and fear to do wrong when they grew to be men.

A cross old man once said to a little boy: " Get out of my way! What are you good for?" The boy answered, "They make men out of such things as we are."

They make men out of such things as we are. And we say to King Alcohol, and his allies, the rumsellers, Tremble tyrants, we shall grow up. Tremble intemperance and rumselling. we shall grow up and put a stop to you by our prayers and votes.

SINGING: " David and Goliath." p. 101.

DIALOGUE between the boys and girls:

Boys. Who hath woe?

Girls. Woe unto him that giveth his neighbor drink. Woe unto them that follow strong drink.

B. Who hath sorrow?

G. They that tarry long at the wine.

B. Who hath contentions?

G. They that go to seek mixed wine.

B. Who hath babblings?

G. Wine is a mocker.

B. Who hath wounds without cause?

G. Strong drink is raging: whosoever is deceived thereby is not wise. Look not thou upon the wine when it is red, when it giveth its color in the cup, when it moveth itself aright.—At the last it biteth like a serpent, and stingeth like an adder.

SINGING, SOLO AND CHORUS: "Bobolink do not drink." p. 68.

Recitation by twenty-six children, arranged in a semi-circle, each one holding up the letter he represents while speaking. (Let the letters be cut out of green card-board.)

> **A** stands for *Alcohol*, a fluid of fire.
> Which often brings death to the seller and buyer.
>
> **B** stands for *Beer*, sometimes sold by the barrel;
> 'Most all who love *it*, love also to quarrel.
>
> **C** is for *Cider ;* in these latter days
> It is called "Satan's kindling." It can make a big blaze.
>
> **D** stands for *Drunkard ;* oh, help him who can
> To reform, be converted, and live like a man!
>
> **E** stands for *Egg-nog*, called an innocent drink;
> Made of milk, eggs, and brandy—is it *innocent*, think?
>
> **F** stands for *Fight*, which is easy for those
> Who of brandy and beer take a liberal dose.

G stands for *Gutter*, and also for *Gin ;*
  Who use much of the *latter* the *former* get in.

H stands for *Hops*, a vine much abused;
  By those who make ale, beer, and porter it's used.

I is for *Idler ;* no work will he do;

J is for *Jug*, his companion and foe.

K is for *Kindness ;* how little is shown
  To those who through liquor have desperate grown!

L is for *Loafer*, who, after much drinking,
  Stands on the corner, apparently thinking.

M stands for *Maniac*, his reason all gone;
  His family heart-broken. Pray, who did the wrong?

N is for *Night*, the time for dark deeds ;

O is for *Outcast*, who on crumbs and husks feeds.

P stands for *Pipes*, which you always will find
  In places where liquor is sold—every kind.

Q *questions* us whether 'tis prudent or wise
  To smoke and to drink. There can be *no disguise.*

R *um* shows itself sooner or later in all ;
  Flee the tempter! Oh, how he'd rejoice in your fall!

S stands for *Station-house*, where, in sad plight,
  Poor drunkards are frequently taken at night.

T for *Tobacco*, used in various ways,
  To rob men of their strength and shorten their days.

U stands for *Usury ;* this *adds* to the woes
  Of rum's victims when to the pawnbroker's he goes.

V is for *Vine ;* its innocent fruit
  Is made to help man sink below the poor brute.

W for *Whiskey*, a very mean drink ;
  When any take to this they very soon sink.

X 's, *one*, *two*, and *three*, are used to describe
  A drink by which many thousands have died.

Y stands for *Youth ;* oh, be wise and beware !
  Yield not to the tempter and die in despair.

Z stands for *Zeal*, which helps us to win
  Many souls from the power of Satan and sin.

                                        Mrs. V. J. Kent.

SINGING: "My Soul be on thy guard." p. 153.

RECITATION BY A LITTLE GIRL:

Have you all wondered to see our little blue bows? (Each child has a tiny blue bow pinned on the left breast). I will tell you the meaning of them. God told the Jews to wear 'a ribbon of blue on the borders of their garments' as a sign that they were God's people, and on their way to Heaven. Our little blue bows are to show these things: 1st, that we are going to live looking up towards Heaven and noble things, rather than down toward the rum bottle and the gutter. 2nd, that we are going to keep ourselves from wicked, intemperate companions. 3rd, that we are going to be temperance folks ourselves, and mean to help others to be so too. 4th, that we want to be known by everyone who sees us as temperance boys and girls.

SINGING : "The Bonnie bit of Blue." p.117,

CHRISTMAS BELLS.

(Hang in a row across the front of the platform eight bells of good size, made of evergreen upon a wire foundation. Have in each one a clear toned bell. Attach a cord to each bell, so that the whole row may be rung by little girls in a sort of merry chimes to begin the service.)

RINGING OF BELLS.

SINGING : "Merry Chiming Bells." p. 11.

SCRIPTURE RECITATION, Luke 2: 8-18.

SINGING: "Jesus in the manger." p. 60.

RECITATION by a very little child, (or it may be sung by a child to the air of "Home, Sweet Home.")

CHILD'S CHRISTMAS HYMN.

Away in a manger,
No crib for his bed,
The little Lord Jesus
    Lay down his sweet head.
The stars in the sky
    Looked down where He lay,
The little Lord Jesus
    Asleep in the hay.

The cattle are lowing,
    The poor baby wakes,
But little Lord Jesus,
    No crying He makes.
I love thee, Lord Jesus,
    Look down from the sky,
And stay by my crib
    Watching my lullaby.

(It was written by Martin Luther for his own children.)

RECITATION (by fifteen little children coming to the platform one by one as each verse is recited, and standing in a row. Each child should have hung about his neck with a ribbon, the letter which he represents, made out of gilt card-board or evergreen.)

THE BABE OF BETHLEHEM.

B stands for *Bible* where we read
About the Saviour whom we need.

A stands for *angels*. How they sing,
About the birth of Christ our King!

B stands for God's *Beloved* Son.
He offers life to every one.

E is for *Egypt* where he fled,
When Herod thought his blood to shed.

O is the *offering* which we bring,
Our hearts we give to Christ our King.

F is for Jesus as our *Friend*;
Whose love for us will never end.

B stands for *Bethlehem*, the town
Where for our sakes the Lord came down.

E is for *Eve*, to whom was given
Promise that Christ would come from Heaven

T is the *tidings* of great joy,
Good news to every girl and boy.

H is the *host* who in the sky
Sung, "Glory be to God on High."

L is *Lord* Jesus, my heart's king,
To whom our gifts to-day we bring.

E is *Emmanuel*. God with us
Who saves us from sin's awful curse.

H is the *Holy*, harmless Child—
I wish I were as meek and mild.

E means *Exalted* is He now;
Before Him every knee shall bow.

M is the *Motto* which we bring,—
The blessed Babe of Bethlehem.

ALL RECITE:

    Our Christmas day long, long ago,
      God gave this Gift to you and me.
    To-day, O, Lord, our love to show
      We give our hearts, ourselves to Thee.

            Adapted from Scholar's Handbook.

SINGING : " Little Children pressing near." p. 98.

RECITATION BY SEVEN GIRLS.—

OUR OFFERINGS.

ALL TOGETHER.
" We, too, would an offering bring,
  Welcome and adore our King."

FIRST GIRL.
" What can *I* give to Jesus
  Who gave Himself for me?
How can I show my love for Him
  Who died on Calvary?"

SECOND GIRL.
" I'll give my *heart* to Jesus,
  In childhood's tender spring;
I know that He will not despise
  So small an offering."

THIRD GIRL.
" I'll give my *soul* to Jesus,
  And calmly, gladly rest
It's youthful hopes and fond desires
  Upon His loving breast."

FOURTH GIRL.
" I'll give my *mind* to Jesus,
  And seek in thoughtful hours
His Spirit's grace to consecrate
  It's early opening powers."

FIFTH GIRL.
" I'll give my *strength* to Jesus,
  Of foot and hand and will;
Run where He sends, and ever strive
  His pleasure to fulfill."

SIXTH GIRL.
" I'll give my *time* to Jesus:
  O, that each hour might be
Filled up with holy love for Him
  Who spent His life for me."

SEVENTH GIRL.
" I'll give my wealth to Jesus:
  'Tis little I possess;
But all I am, and all I have,
  Dear Lord, accept and bless."

COLLECTION AND SONG: " Little Givers come and bring." Songs for Little Folks, p. 81.

SINGING: " Star, Beautiful Star." p. 74.

(Let the first verse be sung as a solo, and the last two as a chorus.)

SCRIPTURE RECITATIONS. Matt. 1: 21. Jno. 3: 16. Acts 4: 12. 2 Tim. 1: 9. Rom. 5: 8. Heb. 9: 24 first cl. 1 Cor. 15: 20 first cl. Jno. 14: 3 (To be given by eight little girls, standing beneath the evergreen bells. Let each little girl ring her bell before giving her recitation, and then let them all be rung sweetly together at the last.)

SINGING: " One Rosy Crown." p. 84.

A CROWN OF FLOWERS. (Let the teacher tell the following story, and then call each child to put a flower into a wire crown.) A little girl was sitting on the grass, weaving a crown of flowers. Her mother asked her for whom she was making it. " It is for Jesus; In Sunday-school I learned about the crown of thorns that the cruel men made for Him, and now I am going to make Him a crown of flowers."

SINGING: " Blessed, Blessed Jesus." p. 91.

Tune—"Old Hundred." L. M.

Praise God from whom all blessings flow;
Praise Him, all creatures here below;
Praise Him above, ye heavenly host;
Praise Father, Son, and Holy Ghost.

Tune—"Sabbath." 7. 6 lines.

1 Safely through another week,
  God has brought us on our way;
Let us now a blessing seek,
  Waiting in His courts to-day,
Day of all the week the best,
Emblem of eternal rest.

2 Here we come Thy name to praise;
  Let us feel Thy presence near;
May Thy glory meet our eyes,
  While we in Thy house appear;
Here afford us Lord a taste
Of our everlasting rest.

Tune—"Watchman." S. M.

1 Once more before we part,
  Oh, bless the Saviour's name;
Let every tongue and every heart
Adore and praise the same.

2 Lord, in Thy grace we came,
  That blessing still impart;
We meet in Jesus' sacred name,
In Jesus' name we part.

Tune—"Sicilian." 8. 7.

Heavenly Father, grant Thy blessing
On the teaching of this day;

That our hearts Thy fear possessing
May from sin be turned away.

Tune—"Downs." C. M.

1 How shall the young secure their hearts,
And guard their lives from sin?
Thy Word the choicest rule imparts
To keep the conscience clean

2 Thy Word is everlasting truth,
How pure in every page!
That holy book shall guide our youth,
And well support our age.

Tune—"Antioch." C. M.

Joy to the world, the Lord is come!
  Let earth receive her King;
Let every heart prepare Him room,
  And heaven and nature sing.

Tune—"Christmas." C. M.

1 While shepherds watched their flocks by night,
All seated on the ground,
The angel of the Lord came down,
And glory shone around.

2 "Fear not," said He, for mighty dread
Had seized their troubled mind,-
"Glad tidings of glad joy I bring
For you and all mankind.

3 "To you in David's town this day,
Is born of David's line,

The Saviour, who is Christ, the
   Lord,
And this shall be the sign;—

4 "The heavenly babe you there
   shall find
To human view displayed,
All meanly wrapped in swathing
   bands,
And in a manger laid.

5 "Thus spoke the seraph and
   forthwith
Appeared a shining throng
Of angels, praising God, who thus
Addressed their cheerful song;—

6 "All glory be to God on high,
And to the earth be peace;
Good will henceforth from heaven
   to men,
Begin, and never cease."

Tune—"Woodland." C. M.

Our sorrows and our sins were laid
On Thee, alone on Thee;
Thy precious blood our ransom
   paid,
Thine all the glory be.

Tune—"Martyrdom." C. M.

1 The head that once was crowned
   with thorns,
Is crowned with glory now;
A royal diadem adorns
The mighty Victor's brow.

2 The highest place that heaven
   affords
Is His by sovereign right;
The King of kings, and Lord of
   lords,
He reigns in glory bright.

Tune—"Horton." 7.

Gracious Spirit, Love divine!
Let Thy light within me shine;
All my guilty fears remove,
Fill me with Thy heavenly love.

Tune—"Kentucky." S. M.

A charge to keep I have,
   A God to glorify,
A never dying soul to save,
   And fit it for the sky.

Tune—"Dennis." S. M.

1 How gentle God's commands!
   How kind His precepts are!
Come, cast your burdens on the
   Lord,
   And trust His constant care.

2 Beneath His watchful eye
   His saints securely dwell;
That hand which bears creation up
   Shall guard His children well.

Tune—"Pleyel's Hymn." 7.

Children of the heavenly King,
As ye journey, sweetly sing;
Sing your Saviour's worthy praise,
Glorious in His works and ways.

Tune—"Ware." L. M.

1 Abide with me from morn till
   eve,
For without Thee I cannot live;
Abide with me when night is nigh,
For without Thee I dare not die.

2 Be near to bless me when I wake,
Ere through the world my way I
   take;
Abide with me when night is nigh,
For without Thee I dare not die.

Tune—"Olivet." 6. 4.

1 My faith looks up to Thee,
Thou Lamb of Calvary,
  Saviour divine!
Now hear me while I pray,
Take all my guilt away,
O let me from this day
  Be wholly Thine.

2 While life's dark maze I tread,
And griefs around me spread,
  Be Thou my Guide;
Bid darkness turn to day,
Wipe sorrow's tears away,
Nor let me ever stray
  From Thee aside.

Tune—"Fulton." 7.

Saviour! teach me day by day,
Love's sweet lesson to obey;
Sweeter lesson cannot be,
Loving Him who first loved me.

Tune—"Nuremburg." 7.

Teach me all Thy steps to trace,
Strong to follow in Thy grace;
Learning how to love from Thee,
Loving Him who first loved me.

Tune—"Laban." S. M.

1 My soul, be on thy guard,
  Ten thousand foes arise;
And hosts of sin are pressing hard
  To draw thee from the skies.

2 Oh, watch and fight and pray!
  The battle ne'er give o'er;
Renew it boldly every day,
  And help divine implore.

Tune—"Oriola." C. M. D.

1 Dear Jesus, let Thy pitying eye
  Look kindly down on me;
A sinful, weak, and helpless child,
  I come Thy child to be.
O blessed Saviour! take my heart,
  This sinful heart of mine,
And wash it clean in every part, ·
  Make me a child of Thine.

2 My sins though great, Thou canst
    forgive,
  For Thou hast died for me;
Amazing love! help me, O God
  Thine own dear child to be.
For Thou hast said, "Forbid them
    not:
  Let children come to Me;"
I hear Thy voice, and now, dear
    Lord,
  I come Thy child to be.

Tune—"Missionary Hymn." 7. 6.

1. From Greenland's icy mountains,
  From India's coral strand,
Where Afric's sunny fountains
  Roll down their golden sand;
From many an ancient river,
  From many a palmy plain,
They call us to deliver
  Their land from error's chain.

2 Shall we whose souls are lighted
  With wisdom from on high,—
Shall we to men benighted
  The lamp of life deny?
Salvation, oh, salvation!
  The joyful sound proclaim,
Till earth's remotest nation
  Has learned Messiah's name.

Tune—"Frederick." 11.

1 I would not live alway; no, welcome the tomb;
Since Jesus hath lain there, I dread not its gloom;
There sweet be my rest till He bid me arise
To hail Him in triumph descending the skies.

2 Who, who would live alway, away from His God,
Away from yon heaven, that blissful abode,
Where the rivers of pleasure flow o'er the bright plains,
And the noontide of glory eternally reigns.

Tune—"Wilmot." 8. 7.

1 Day by day the little daisy
Looks up with its yellow eye,
Never murmurs, never wishes
It were hanging up on high.

2 And the air is just as pleasant,
And as bright the sunny sky,
To the daisy by the footpath
As to flowers that bloom on high.

3 God has given to each his station,
Some have riches and high place,
Some have lowly homes and labor,—
All may have His precious grace.

4 And God loveth all His children
Rich, and poor, and high, and low,

And they all shall meet in heaven
Who have served Him here below.

Tune—"Ortonville." C. M.

1 Lord, I would own Thy tender care
And all Thy love to me;
The food I eat, the clothes I wear,
Are all bestowed by Thee.

2 'Tis Thou preservest me from death,
And dangers every hour,
I cannot draw another breath
Unless Thou give me power.

3 Such goodness, Lord, and constant care
A child can ne'er repay;
But may it be my daily prayer
To love Thee and obey.

Tune—"America." 6. 4.

1 My country! 'tis of thee,
Sweet land of liberty,
Of thee I sing:
Land where my fathers died!
Land of the Pilgrim's pride!
From every mountain side
Let freedom ring!

2 Our father's God! to thee,
Author of liberty,
To Thee we sing:
Long may our land be bright,
With freedom's holy light,
Protect us by Thy might,
Great God, our King!

HYMNS.

Tune—" Rockingham." L. M.

I know that my Redeemer lives;
What joy the blest assurance gives!
He lives, He lives, who once was
   dead;
He lives, my everlasting Head!

2 He lives to bless me with His love;
He lives, to plead for me above;
He lives, my hungry soul to feed;
He lives, to help in time of need.

3 He lives, and grants me daily
   breath;
He lives, and I shall conquer death;
He lives, my mansion to prepare;
He lives, to bring me safely there,

4 He lives, all glory to His name;
He lives, my Saviour, still the same;
What joy the blest assurance gives,
I know that my Redeemer lives!

Tune—" Believer." C. M.

How sweet the name of Jesus
   sounds
In a believer's ear!
It soothes his sorrows, heals his
   wounds,
And drives away his fear.

2 It makes the wounded spirit
   whole,
And calms the troubled breast;
'Tis manna to the hungry soul,
And to the weary rest.

3 Jesus, my Shepherd, Saviour,
   Friend,
My Prophet, Priest, and King,
My Lord, my Life, my Way, my End,
Accept the praise I bring!

Tune—" Onward." 6, 5.

Onward, Christian soldiers!
  Marching as to war,
With the cross of Jesus
  Going on before.
Christ, the royal Master,
  Leads against the foe;
Forward into battle,
  See His banners go!
    Onward, Christian soldiers!
    Marching as to war,
    With the cross of Jesus
    Going on before.

2 Onward, then, ye people!
  Join our happy throng,
Blend with ours your voices
  In the triumph-song;
Glory, laud, and honor
  Unto Christ the King,
This through countless ages
  Men and angels sing.

Tune—" He Leadeth Me." L. M.

He leadeth me! O blessed thought!
O words with heavenly comfort
   fraught!
Whate'er I do, where'er I be,
Still 'tis God's hand that leadeth
   me.
He leadeth me, He leadeth me,
By His own hand He leadeth me:
His faithful follower I would be,
For by His hand He leadeth me.

Tune—" Pleyel's Hymn." 7

Sing we to our God above,
Praise eternal as His love,
Praise him, all ye heavenly host,
Father, Son, and Holy Ghost!

DIRECTIONS FOR MOTION SONGS.

"LITTLE BIRD, YOU ARE WELCOME."—Page 118.

A story or conversation should introduce this game, to the effect that a mother is absent, and sends her love and a letter, by a carrier-pigeon, to her children. A child is chosen to be the pigeon, and when an older person is present, she is chosen to be the mother, who is outside the ring, and sends the letter. The tune may be played or hummed, without words, while the carrier-pigeon flies outside the ring. When the words " Little bird you are welcome" commence, the arms are raised to signify that all windows are open, and the bird flies into the ring and sings the second verse, after which it may give the letter to one of the children. All the children wave their hands, and sing the message to their mother; and at the words " Fly away," the pigeon leaves the ring again and flies back to the mother.

"BIRDIES IN THE WOOD."—Page 119.

While singing the first verse, the children who are chosen to be " Birds" fly about the wood, which is represented by the other children standing in a ring, and holding their arms up in imitation of the branches of the trees.

During the second verse, the birds collect materials to build a nest. which may be formed by two or three others, who join hands and kneel on the floor.

If the ring is large. several nests may be formed, and the number of birds be increased accordingly.

When the third verse begins, the birds come into the nest and close their eyes.

"THE CHICKENS."—Page 120.

One child is chosen by the teacher to feed the chickens, who come hopping and running when they are called; one of the tallest little girls may be the hen, who heads the brood. She sees that all are cared for when picking up their food; then she calls them all around her, and covers them with her wings,

While the group is asleep, the last verse may be sung, or silence may be kept, or the teacher may tell the children, in a soft voice, some interesting fact about the affection of the hen for her chickens.

If the circle is large, several other children may be engaged in representing a farm-yard and a gate at which stands the child who is going to feed the chickens.

" RAIN DROPS."—Page 124.

This piece should be performed in a declamatory style, i,e, the rhythm should be secondary to the emphasis of the words. Let each word be sung naturally and fall into such rhythm as it will. Especially the words " Just like—just like—little—Lottie," should be sung in a hesitating manner, regardless of exact time.

"THE TREES."—Page 128.

An avenue of two rows of children is formed. The arms are held up to represent branches of trees, all of which should have names.
First the trees are gently moved by the breeze: while singing the second verse they move forwards and backwards more violently, and during the third verse they shake their leaves from the branches when the storm is said to be very great.

" SEE MY LITTLE BIRDIE'S NEST."—Page 128.

The child's hands form a nest, in which the ball represents the egg; but it will soon be seen that the importance of the game does not lie in the game itself, (for the hands are kept still) but in the fact that the child learns to respect the life and happiness of even dumb animals.
Kindness to animals should be taught early, by word, example, and practice; for if this be neglected, we cannot wonder if stones are thrown at birds, nests robbed, insects tortured, and cats, dogs, horses, and donkeys ill-treated.

"THE WIND MILL."—Page 129.

Four children join their right hands and stretch the left arm to imitate the arms of the wind-mill. When the song commences, they go round the imaginary axis, indicated by the joined hands. The children in the ring may move their hands either joined or loose, to represent the wind. Although the arms of the mill do not turn both ways, it is well that the children should change and join the left hand, so as to prevent giddiness.

"BLIND FOLDED."—Page 130.

The game " Blind-folded " indicates how the hearing is to be trained without the help of the eye. First, the children go round and sing the verse, while the blind-folded child in the middle listens: then he hands a stick to a child in the ring, which has again been formed at the end of the verse. Now the chosen child may either repeat the tune without words, sing some other song, or imitate the cry of an animal, and, by the voice, the blind-folded child must guess who it is.

"LOOK AT THE CLOCKS."—Page 133.

Let the hands be moved from right to left, and back again to imitate the moving of the pendulum while singing " Tic tac."

158

INDEX.

Titles in SMALL CAPS.—First lines in Roman.

Page.

Abide with me from morn...... 152
A charge to keep I have..... 152
A CHRISTMAS CAROL............. 88
All our little heart-aches.............21
All things bright and beautiful..... 54
ALONE WITH JESUS................. 95
And Jesus said.................... 62
A WONDERFUL HOUSE HAVE I....... 82

BIRDIES IN THE WOOD........... 119
BLESSED, BLESSED JESUS..... 9
BLINDFOLDED....................... 130
Bobolink, do not drink............. 68
BOOK OF GRACE.................... 107
BRIGHTLY GLOWS THE DAY.......... 132

CAROL, SWEETLY CAROL......... 111
CHANT FOR EASTER............115
CHANTS..............58, 62, 113, 115 116
CHILDREN COME 72
CHILDREN MAY COME............. 22
Children of the heavenly King..... 152
CHILDREN'S THANKS.............. 67
CHILD'S PRAYER 12
Christ our passover is sacrificed.... 115
Clap your hands rejoicing.......... 104
CLOSING CHANT.................... 116
COME LEARN OF THE MEEK.......... 44
COME, LEARN THE WAY 42
CRADLE SONG...................... 18

DAVID AND GOLIATH........... 101
DAY BY DAY............. 75
Day by day the glorious sun........ 58
Day by day the little daisy......... 154
Day by day we magnify Thee 75
Dear Jesus, ever at my side....... 39
Dear Jesus, let Thy pitying eye.... 153
Dear little dove, when I think... .. 65
Dear Saviour, ere we part 116
DEAR SAVIOUR, MAY THY BLESSING.. 27

Page.

EARLY, O MY SAVIOUR........... 29
EASTER CAROL................ 64
EASTER SONG...................... 87
Ever blessed Jesus................. 92
Every lily in the meadow.......... 73

FALLING, FALLING, EVER FALLING 112
FAR AWAY.................... 109
Father above. Thou God of love.... 12
Father lead Thy little children..... 34
Fly away pretty moth to your home 36
FOLLOW ME.......... 56
From Greenland's icy mountains... 153

GLORIA PATRI................... 113
Glory be to the Father....... 113
GLORY TO THE FATHER GIVE........ 20
GOD CAN SEE ME EVERY DAY 35
God cares for every little child..... 66
GOD ENTRUSTS TO ALL.............. 40
GOD HAS MADE ALL THINGS......... 54
GOD IS ALWAYS NEAR ME........... 134
GOD IS IN HEAVEN................. 108
GOD'S BLESSED BOOK.............. 31
GOD SPEED THE RIGHT.............. 135
GO TO SLEEP MY DARLING BABY...... 125
Gracious Spirit, Love divine 152
GUARD, MY CHILD, THY TONGUE..... 59

HAPPY CHILDREN.............. 77
HAPPY LITTLE PILGRIMS 7
HAPPY WE, YOUNG AND FREE........ 14
HARK! THE LARK IS SINGING........ 16
Hark! the lilies whisper 106
HARK! THE VOICE.................. 30
Heavenly Father, grant Thy 151
He Leadeth me! O blessed thought. 155
HERE AND THERE.................... 58
HE WHO WOULD LEAD (round)...... 121
HOSANNA......................... 48
Hosanna in the highest............. 48

www.ingramcontent.com/pod-product-compliance
Lightning Source LLC
Chambersburg PA
CBHW020554270326
41927CB00006B/835